The HUNGRY HUNTER

Complete VENISON COOK BOOK

EDITED BY JAMES R. WILSON

Y0-CDF-260

Cover, book, and logos designed by Lenz Design & Communications, Atlanta, GA.

Cover and author photo by Richard T. Bryant

Cover knife and custom rifle made by Jack Crockford

Illustrations by Philip Neugebauer

First Edition Printing by Guest Printing, Athens, Georgia

© **1994 by The Georgia Wildlife Federation**, 1930 Iris Drive, Conyers, GA 30207. All Rights Reserved. This book, or any portion thereof, may not be reproduced in any form, except for review purposes, without the written permission of the author or publisher.

Published by **Georgia Wildlife Press**, The Georgia Wildlife Federation, 1930 Iris Drive, Conyers, Georgia 30207. 1-404-929-3350.

ISBN 0-9644522-0-0 14.95

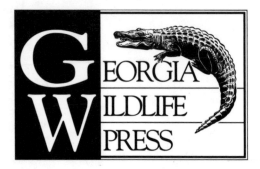

DEDICATION

This book is dedicated to those men, women, boys and girls who go afield in search of the elusive white-tailed deer. It is for those who seek to understand the mysteries of its habits and its place in nature's complex web of life. They are both inspired by its sylvan majesty, and concerned by its modern day plight.

With the rapid disappearance of wildlife habitat as the ever-increasing population of man demands more and more land be converted from its natural state, there is progressively less room for all wild creatures including the white-tailed deer. Unless this trend can be halted, many animals will become the stuff of books and not the wonders of the fields and forests.

It is for those who truly value these animals to become their first line of defense.

CONTENTS

ACKNOWLEDGMENTS

We would like to thank all those people who have contributed their time, various skills and even recipes to this book and have gotten others to contribute as well. Without their efforts, there would be no book. *Special thanks to:*

Hilda Abbott
Devra Anderson
Ren Anderson
Richard T. Bryant
Susan Chapman
Carol Coons
Clay Coons
Scott Crawford
Fio Crockford
Jack Crockford
Ron Curty
Charlotte Dixon
Lou Greathouse
Tommy Gregors
Dorothy Gunn
Bob Hane
James P. Hayes
Misty Herrin
Brenda Humphrey
Jan Ison
Ron James
Carol Johnson
Terry L. Joyner

Richard J. Lenz
John R. Lenz
Sonny Marsh
Ann Mathews
Jerry McCollum
Larry Michaels
Tom Micheli
Charlie Miller
Phillip Neugebauer
Ken O'Shields
Glenn Reeves
Art Rilling
Doug Rithmire
Nancy Rithmire
Larry Speir
Terry Tatum
R.J. "Frenchy" Fecteau
Wydeene Webb
Bobby G. Wesley
Martha White
Anne Wiley
Saskia Mireille Wilson

INTRODUCTION

This first in the projected series of Hungry Hunter Cookbooks from Georgia Wildlife Press deals only with venison. When the term venison is used, it usually refers to any of the common deer-like animals, various species of deer, elk, antelope and moose. When talking about venison in terms of cooking (with this cookbook), meat from any of these animals can be used with one slight exception. Moose is not exactly the same. Moose meat is more highly marbled, more fat streaked in the meat, and is somewhat higher in water content than the other three animals, so it needs less oil in preparation and won't dry out quite as fast in either the freezer or during cooking. It is not a great difference; it's still not like beef, but take it into account when using moose in any of the recipes. While we have tried to concentrate on recipes that are relatively simple, we've also mixed in some that will take more preparation, but we feel are definitely worth the time and result in dishes you will enjoy and be proud to serve to your family and guests. Someone has expended a lot of effort and money getting the meat to the kitchen, so it is worth a little extra time to prepare it properly.

There are hundreds of thousands of deer hunters in the U.S. and a commensurate number of deer taken each year that end up on the kitchen table. It is no accident that today wild deer herds across the country continue to thrive and grow in number. It is due to wise wildlife resource management and ethical hunters who pay in large part for that management through the purchase of hunting licenses and the payment of taxes on hunting equipment. There is an abundance of deer in spite of those persons who would violate those very game laws that have resulted in deer being available in such large numbers. There is no excuse for those people and responsible hunting and non-hunting citizens should do everything in their power to bring them to justice. There are also organizations out there whose avowed purpose it is to put an end to hunting (and fishing and trapping and keeping house pets). I must admit to a very simplistic view of such people. When they are willing to discuss the matter on a biological and realistic basis, I am interested in what they have to say. If they insist on a strictly emotional, irrational approach ignoring the way the natural world works, I am too busy. They have done and will undoubtedly continue to do mental and physical damage through acts of terrorism, but I don't think they will ever have the wide public support they would like us to believe.

We think there is a great need and interest in such a publication as this, so we have given it our best effort. "Our best effort" means the efforts of dozens of folks who have donated the recipes that make up the book itself. All of the recipes have come from them. There have been so many received that I have made no effort to attribute a particular recipe to a particular person. This also means that I have not personally tested or tasted them all, but I've been through many. I'm looking forward to getting to the rest of them. I am sure there are hundreds of variations on these recipes and hundreds more we have never heard of. If you have some favorites that are on the missing list, send them to me at the press. We would love to be able to put out a Hungry Hunter Venison Cookbook, Volume Two and acknowledge your creative cooking, too. I hope you enjoy the book.

James R. Wilson
Marietta, Georgia

GENERAL GUIDELINES ON COOKING VENISON

The biggest mistake most cooks make when preparing venison is to assume they need to make some sort of burnt offering or singed sacrifice to the god of the forest. Overcooking is the worst thing one can do to venison. I've known dozens of persons who like their steaks "burned". O.K., if that's how you think beef is best, but venison should be cooked only half as much as beef and a little less than that is even better. This translates to rare or medium rare. On a meat thermometer, that's about 130-140 degrees Fahrenheit. Remember that venison is a very lean and delicate meat so don't overcook it unless you like your meat the texture and flavor of an inner tube, because that is just what overcooking will give you. Like all other red meats, venison should not be cooked directly from the freezer — or even the refrigerator. Allow it to reach room temperature first, around 70 degrees Fahrenheit. That will help maximize the true flavor. Never thaw frozen venison in a microwave oven as it drives out a great deal of the little moisture there is, resulting in dry, tough meat. If you are in that much of a hurry, open a can of beans. No matter how you cook it, trim all the fat off the outside of the cut of meat you're using. Cooked venison fat doesn't taste good and doesn't do anything for the cooking process either. There will also be a thin dry layer on the surface of the meat after it has aged. Remove that as well. Salting venison before cooking tends to make it tough and it dehydrates the meat. Hold off on the salt until later in the process. When roasting venison, it is necessary to "lard" it somehow. That technique can be accomplished in a couple of ways. The best way is to part with a few dollars and get a large larding needle from a specialty cooking store. This allow you to get additional fat into the venison. Often pork fat or even bacon is used because it is easy to get, but other heavier fats will work just as well and are usually available from a butcher. If you only have a knife, you can make deep cuts in the meat and push the fat in manually. If you are roasting venison, put it in a hot oven (500 degrees Fahrenheit) for about fifteen minutes to sear it. Then the temperature can be turned to a roasting temperature of 300-350 degrees Fahrenheit and cooked for about twenty minutes per pound. A meat thermometer should insure that it is not being overcooked. Another good idea is to not poke cooking venison with a fork. It already has a limited amount of moisture, so don't punch holes in it to let out what little there is. The only exception to this is the larding process which adds moisture and is worth punching a hole for. Herbs and spices are used in cooking almost every cut of meat. That holds for venison, too, but go lighter on them than you would on heavier meats like beef. It doesn't really take much for venison. The basic spices that go with about all red meat are thyme, marjoram, basil, oregano and rosemary. Fresh herbs are always better (more potent and tasty) than the dried variety, but if you can only find the latter, a rule of thumb is that a 1/4 teaspoon of dried herbs equals about one teaspoon of fresh. Finally, with the exceptions of those special characteristics of venison (less fat, etc), it is worth experimenting with a variety of recipes that call for beef and not venison. Obviously you need to make allowances for the differences now that you know what they are, but you certainly can come up with a lot of new dishes on your own by being a little adventurous and creative. ■

FRYING PAN INSURANCE:

EARLY CARE OF VENISON

There are two comments about early care you need to keep in mind. First, when a hunter takes a deer in the field, it should be with one shot culminating in an instant kill. The foremost reason for this is that it is the humane thing to do. If you doubt you can get the one shot kill, don't take the chance. There is always another day, another deer. Nowadays it is rare that one is hunting for critical subsistence, so keep your ethics high. Secondly, a wounded deer will run, making its muscles tense and spreading adrenaline through its body. The result will be meat that is much tougher. Some people claim that the adrenaline also effects the taste of the venison, but I don't know how that can be proven or gauged given all the other variables including age and condition of the animal and cooking techniques. If your venison is taken in the field, as opposed to being purchased in a specialty meat shop (of which there are a growing number due to game farming), the most important thing is to get the meat cooled as soon as possible. This means getting the carcass open and emptied so that cooling can occur from the inside out and not just from the outside.

It's beyond the scope of this book to give a detailed account of how to empty a deer. It used to be that one would be referred to a good book on the subject, but now there are good videos on market. If a picture is worth 10,000 words, a moving picture has got to be worth even more. The next step is skinning and it's tempting to write a long section in this book on the perfect way to skin a deer. The problem is, I don't think there is one perfect way. I've seen deer hung by the feet, by the neck and by the horns as well as skinned on the ground starting on either end or the top or bottom. Every one of those ways worked fine — as long as the skinners remembered the single, simplest thing; if they remembered what they are supposed to have when the task is finished. You're supposed to have hide and meat with neither one attached to the other. I don't think there is anything worse than to see a couple of people attack a deer to skin it and end up with a hide that (1) is full of holes where the knife "slipped" and there is hide left on the meat; (2) is streaked with lean red meat where the knife "slipped" the other direction and meat is left on the hide; and (3) is thrown in a ditch because of one or both of these circumstances and "wasn't any good." Every effort should be made to save the hide. Either you can tan it or you can have it professionally tanned or give it to someone else who will make good use of it. The best, but not the easiest or quickest way to get the hide off cleanly, is to ball your fist and roll it between the hide and the meat, separating the two, while pulling the hide off. If you're working with a skinning knife, the operative word is patience. Take your time and do it right. After all, you already have a lot of hours and dollars invested in just getting a deer to skin.

Anyone who has partially processed meat in the field knows what a mistake it is to get dirt, leaves or any other type of debris on the skinned meat. Not only is it unsanitary, it is almost impossible to get off. If somehow this happens and it's necessary to clean off the outside of meat, use vinegar and not water. Water will tend to toughen the meat. This is especially true if you need to clean out the inside of the carcass. A small sponge or lint free cloth (in that order of preference) can be used for this process. Note that we're talking about wiping off the meat, not soaking it off. I have seen some hunters bring their deer meat from the field in coolers full of cold water. While this does cool the meat, it also toughens it and is not recommended. Some sort of ice has to be added to the cooler for transport, just be sure as it melts that the cold water doesn't come in contact with the meat. Venison is known not to be high in moisture content which means you need to preserve as much of that moisture as possible. The sooner you can either cook it or freeze it, the better. You should always freeze the meat in the size package you intend to use completely and right away. One meal (for any number of people), one package. Keep in mind that the smaller the package, however, the easier it is to dry out in the freezer, so store in the largest size package it's feasible to cook. Perhaps you can cook a couple of dishes at one time from a larger package and eat the second cooked dish a day or two later after having just stored it in the refrigerator. Venison won't keep forever in the freezer. Even if you have it perfectly wrapped and you freeze it immediately, you're pushing it if you keep it from one season to the next. What you lose is moisture and that translates to flavor loss. You've probably noticed that even an ice cube evaporates to nothing if you leave it too long in the freezer. The same is true of moisture in frozen meat (or anything else). For freezing, double wrap the meat in freezer paper with the shiny side against the meat. The object is to keep as much air as possible away from the venison thus preventing freezer burn. Assuming that it is not freezer burned (white and shrivelled looking) over a long period of time, you will still be able to eat the venison that has been frozen that long, but don't expect to get the fine flavor and don't blame meat. If you need to keep the meat a longer time, look into one of the jerky recipes offered in this book. Even then, remember that there are limits. If you eat all your venison before the next season, eat the turkey or fish you caught the following spring while it is still fresh. With reasonable care in storage and preparation, venison will be some of the best eating you or your guests have ever experienced. ■

"HEALTH" INSURANCE:

THE NUTRITIONAL QUALITIES OF VENISON

By P. Susan Chapman MS, RD, LD, Registered Dietitian

Venison is an excellent addition to a healthy diet. The low-fat content of the meat is a key factor. Using less fat in our diet can help in the prevention of several health problems. Because of the low-fat content, venison stores well. And best of all, it is free from drugs that potentially taint the meat of domestic animals.

When compared to other wild and domestic meats, antelope and deer are the leanest. (See chart on page 19.) The amount of fat in venison varies from season to season, to the age of the animal, and even location of the cut of meat on the carcass. (Values in the chart represent an average value.)

Deer are fattest in early autumn at the end of the most plentiful feeding season. The older animal, in general, will be fatter than the young. The most exercised muscles, as in domestic meat, are the leanest cuts. In deer as in cattle, the front leg and shoulder muscles are leaner then the back leg muscles. The tenderer cuts are usually less-used, fattier muscles. The best blend of lean and tender are the cuts from the rib, rib eye roasts, tenderloin and rib eye steaks.

Since venison is very lean overall, it fits into any healthy eating plan and in some cases, special diets needed to treat illnesses. The general U.S. Dietary Guidelines include reducing the fat and cholesterol in our diet as a goal. The average American has a diet where 45 to 50 percent of the calories come from fat. It is not surprising to see that most of the domestic meats we use are very high in fat. The chart shows a comparison of domestic meat versus game.

A portion of venison could have as little as 16 to 18 percent of the calories from fat. Most of the recipes included in this cookbook have added fat in the form of oil, margarine and sometimes butter. Some of the fat could be eliminated by using no-stick cooking spray to pan fry the meat. In other recipes, the amounts of oil and margarine can be reduced by one fourth to one half without affecting the quality of the recipes. In any case, calories from fat will most often be 30 percent or less when starting with such a lean main ingredient.

The American Heart Association has more specific guidelines for fat and cholesterol in the diet. The goal for someone with heart problems is to keep the total fat in the diet to 30% or less. The daily goal for cholesterol in the diet is 300 milligrams (mg) or less. The amounts of cholesterol found in game and domestic meat is virtually the same. The dramatic difference comes when comparing the low fat meat from deer and antelope to the supposedly low fat beef and chicken. Venison has one third the fat of lean ground beef and light meat chicken. It is easier to meet the American Heart Association guidelines for fat and cholesterol by using venison in place of domestic meats.

The high fat and cholesterol in the American diet needs to be reduced to prevent fatty buildup in our blood vessels. The fatty deposits or plaque, cause a narrowing of the veins and arteries. This in turn causes high blood pressure and poor circulation. Blood flow can be interrupted because of the thick fatty deposits. When this occurs it can be the cause of a heart attack or a stroke. These diseases are prevalent in the United States because our diets include so much high fat domestic beef and pork, and dairy products and eggs.

Diabetics are directed to keep the fat in their diet as low as possible. Someone who has diabetes is more prone to circulation and heart problems. Venison is a tasty, low-fat, low-calorie choice that will improve the variety in a somewhat limited diet. We have included diabetic exchanges for each of the recipes to help in using these cooking suggestions for a person with diabetes.

The low-fat meat will help keep the total fat in the diet down but will also help in weight control. Many Americans and adult-type (Type II) diabetics are overweight. The main means of preventing and controlling this type diabetes is to reduce to a good body weight. High-fat ground beef which can have 50 to 60 percent calories from fat can be easily replaced with a lean ground venison that is only 16 to 18 percent fat. Reducing fat means reducing calories which leads to losing weight. Small changes like this can be made painlessly but can result in several pounds of weight lost for the overweight person.

Portion sizes are something to consider when discussing a healthy diet. Meat portions need only be 3 to 4 ounces in size. Keep this in mind when specifying the packaging of the meat at time of butchering. The packaging should be done in consideration of how much meat would be prepared at one time. Considering that the meat portions may be smaller than what you are accustomed to, the venison supply will last much longer.

The deer meat does keep well when frozen because of its low-fat content. The fat in the meat can turn rancid even when frozen. Freezing the meat slows down but doesn't stop these changes. Other wild game and domestic meats — because of the high fat content — do not keep as well for as long.

There are many other health reasons to follow a low-fat diet of which venison can be a critical ingredient. The low-fat diet may prevent the onset of multiple sclerosis (MS). Fat in the diet is implicated as a contributing factor to many forms of cancer. As you can see this cookbook can help you and your family to a healthier low-fat lifestyle.

A new and growing concern for using domestic meat in the diet is the use of antibiotics and steroids in the treatment and growth of domestic animals. There are fears that antibiotics and steroids may still be present in the meat we eat. Since this is not tested in the inspection of domestic meat, we don't know how much is present and therefore don't know what impact this has on our overall health. The advantage of eating wild game is that you avoid the possibility of drug-tainted meat in your diet.

As you discover the new tastes suggested by this cookbook, you can enjoy them free of guilt and worry. Each recipe includes an analysis of calories, protein, and fat per serving if your have any doubt. Remember you are starting with a delicious low-fat main ingredient that is a wonderful addition to any diet. ■

REFERENCES:

American Diabetic Association. 1992. Manual of Clinical Diabetics. Chicago. American Diabetic Association.

Cooper, K. 1988. Controlling Cholesterol. New York: Bantam Books.

Herbert, V., Subak-Sharpe, G., and Hammonk, D. 1990. The Mount Sinai School of Medicine Complete Book of Nutrition. New York: St. Martin's Press.

National Research Council. 1989. Recommended Dietary Allowances. Washington, D.C. : National Academy Press.

Pennington, J. 1994. Food Values of Portions Commonly Used. Philadelphia: J.B. Lippencott Company.

Stevenson, J.M., Seman, D.L. and Littlejohn, R.P. 1992. Seasonal variation in venison quality of mature, farmed red deer stags in New Zealand. Journal of Animal Science. 70(5): 1389.

Fat Comparison of Game and Domestic Meats

Meat	Grams Fat	Mg. Cholesterol	Percent Cal.'s From Fat
GAME			
Deer	3.2	112	18
Antelope	2.7	126	16
Rabbit	3.5	123	18
Squirrel	4.7	121	25
Bass	4.7	87	29
Catfish	4.2	57	33
Trout	6.6	57	40
Salmon	8.1	70	40
Quail	4.5	n/a	30
Duck	28.4	84	76
Goose	21.9	91	65
DOMESTIC			
Beef Brisket	10.1	93	42
Beefalo	6.3	58	30
Regular Ground Beef	20.9	87	66
Lean Ground Beef	16.1	82	58
Beef Prime Rib	33.2	85	76
Pork Sausage	27.2	64	78
Pork Loin	27.9	102	68
Veal Loin	17.2	118	55
Chicken Dark Meat	15.8	91	56
Chicken Light Meat	10.9	84	44

n/a not available, Mg. = milligrams
Values represent a 3.5 ounce portion are for items cooked without added fat.

Recipe Nutritional Notes:

Recipes are calculated to an approximate 4-ounce portion of meat when serving size not specified. The nutrient content of recipes may vary depending on products and methods used in preparation. The following abbreviations are used in the nutritional breakdowns: "Pro" for protein and "CHO" for carbohydrates. Diabetics should consult their doctor or the American Diabetes Association for information on how to use meal exchanges.

NOTES

_____

_____

_____

_____

_____

_____

_____

_____

_____

CUTLETS & RIBS

Venison Spareribs

Calories: 210
Pro: 36
Fat: 6
CHO: 0

Diabetic Exchanges:
Lean Meat: 4
Vegetable: 0
Bread: 0

12 venison ribs
1 cup chili sauce
1/2 cup sherry
1 stalk celery, chopped

salt and pepper
1/2 cup lemon juice
1 onion, chopped
1/2 green pepper, chopped

Cut ribs into serving sized pieces. Arrange ribs in roasting pan and brown, uncovered in a hot oven (400 degrees) for about 20 minutes. Drain off any fat. Combine all remaining ingredients in saucepan and bring to a boil. Pour over ribs. Reduce heat to 325 degrees and bake, covered, for about 2 1/2 hours or until tender. While cooking baste often with white wine or water. Serves 4.

Marinated Leg of Venison

Calories: 240
Pro: 34
Fat: 8
CHO: 3

Diabetic Exchanges:
Lean Meat: 4-5
Vegetable: 0
Bread: 0

4-5 pounds leg of venison
2 cups red wine
2 bay leaves
2 teaspoons dry mustard
3 tablespoons flour
1/2 cup paw-paw jelly

4 slices bacon
1/2 cup olive oil
4 cloves garlic, minced
1 teaspoon salt
1 teaspoon coarsely ground
   black pepper

Marinate the venison 24 hours before you plan to cook it. This is a must. Place the leg of venison in a deep bowl. Combine the wine, bay leaves, dry mustard, olive oil, garlic, salt and pepper, and pour over the venison. Cover with foil and refrigerate 24 hours, turning the meat several times. Preheat the oven to 450 degrees. Drain the venison and reserve the marinade. Place the meat on a rack in a shallow pan and cover with bacon. Roast for 30 minutes, basting several times with the marinade, then reduce the heat to 350 degrees and continue to roast another hour. After the venison is done, put on a platter and keep warm. Set the roasting pan over a burner, add the flour to the drippings, and cook until it is browned. Strain the reserved marinade and stir into the pan, cooking until smooth and well thickened. Add the paw-paw jelly; cook only until the jelly is melted and blended with the sauce. Serves 6-8.

Venison Cutlets

Calories: 284	Diabetic Exchanges:
Pro: 35	Lean Meat: 4
Fat: 8	Vegetable: 0
CHO: 18	Bread: 1
2 pounds venison steak	**flour**
2 tablespoons butter	**salt and pepper**
2/3 cup sour cream	**celery salt**
Heinz 57 sauce	**bay leaf**

Cut venison into individual cutlets and roll in well seasoned flour. Melt butter in iron skillet and brown cutlets on both sides over medium heat. When nicely browned pour sour cream over cutlets and season with salt and pepper, Heinz 57 sauce, celery salt and bay leaf. Cover skillet and simmer about an hour over low heat or until tender. Serve over hot steamed rice. Serves 6-8.

Venison Californie

Calories: 200
Pro: 36
Fat: 5
CHO: 4

Diabetic Exchanges:
Lean Meat: 3
Vegetable: 1
Bread: 0

2 cups wine vinegar
1 clove garlic
1 teaspoon oregano
1 whole clove
4 strips salt pork
2 large onions, sliced
1 cup peas, fresh, frozen or canned
1 cup white table wine (Dry Muscat or Sauterne)

4 cups water
3 tablespoons chopped
   parsley
4 pounds venison chops,
   steaks or ribs
1 cup diced carrots

Combine vinegar and water and bring to boil; add garlic, parsley, clove and oregano. Cool. Pour into glass or porcelain container. Place venison in this marinade and refrigerate overnight. Turn occasionally. When ready to cook, remove venison from marinade and dry off with paper towels. In heavy kettle or dutch oven, fry salt pork lightly, then put in venison and top with onion slices. Cook over moderate heat about 30 minutes until meat is well browned on both sides. Add vegetables plus a small amount of liquid from canned peas or some of the strained marinade. Bake, covered in a slow oven (300 degrees) about 1 1/2 hours. When meat is tender, add wine and continue cooking another 15 minutes. Serves 12.

WHITE-TAILED DEER FAWNS ARE USUALLY BORN IN MAY AND WEIGH APPROXIMATELY 4 POUNDS AT BIRTH.

Roast Leg of Venison

Calories: 335
Pro: 36
Fat: 11
CHO: 23

Diabetic Exchanges:
Lean Meat: 4
Vegetable: 1
Bread: 1

Marinade mixture for venison:
1 leg of venison
1 teaspoon white pepper
1/2 cup chopped scallions
1/2 cup olive oil
1 1/2 cups red wine
1 cup teriyaki sauce
1 teaspoon salt
3 bay leaves
2 cloves garlic, crushed
3 cups hot water
1/2 cup red wine vinegar

Vegetables:
3-4 baking potatoes, peeled and cut into eighths
1 cup celery cut diagonally into 1/2" pieces
1 cup carrots, peeled and sliced
1 medium onion, sliced
8 slices of bacon
4 tablespoons corn starch mixed in 1/2 cup of water

Scrub venison well with vinegar and dry with a paper towel. Mix all marinade, pour over the leg, and cover. Marinate for 8 hours, turning occasionally. Remove from marinade and in a roasting pan place in a 375 degree oven, covered. Cook 45 minutes. At the end of this time, uncover, arrange slices of bacon on top of the leg, turn the oven down to 350 degrees and cook for 60 minutes. Baste the leg frequently during this time. Remove the bay leaves and skim off any excess fat from the liquid. Stir in cornstarch mixture and cook for several minutes to make gravy.

> # THE ANCESTORS OF OUR MODERN DEER HAD FIVE TOES.

Fried Venison Cutlet

Calories: 360
Pro: 39
Fat: 14
CHO: 22

Diabetic Exchanges:
Lean Meat: 4
Vegetable: 0
Bread: 1 1/2

4 venison cutlets, 2 pounds
1/2 cup olive oil
1/2 cup lemon juice
1 teaspoon salt
4 tablespoons currant jelly
1/2 teaspoon freshly ground pepper

1/2 cup flour
1 egg
3/4 cup dry bread crumbs
4 tablespoons butter or
  margarine

Marinate the cutlets in a mixture of olive oil and lemon juice for several hours, turning to make sure that all pieces get equally marinated. Remove and drain the meat. Dredge the pieces in the flour and lightly salt and pepper. Beat the egg in a shallow bowl. Dip the meat in the egg, then in the dry bread crumbs. In a large skillet, melt the butter and saute the cutlets about 5 minutes per side or until brown. Place the cutlets on a heated serving dish. Spoon the currant jelly into the drippings in the skillet, scraping the bottom to blend in all the drippings. Bring to a boil, then pour over the meat on the serving dish. Serve immediately. Serves 8.

Barbecued Venison Chops

Calories: 215
Pro: 36
Fat: 4
CHO: 10

Diabetic Exchanges:
Lean Meat: 3
Vegetable: 1
Bread: 0

6 venison loin chops, 1 inch thick
  6 ounces each

2 tablespoons peanut oil
1/4 cup lemon juice

1/4 cup Worcestershire sauce   1/2 onion, finely chopped
1 teaspoon garlic, finely chopped   1/2 teaspoon ground pepper
3 tomatoes, pureed   1 cup dark beer
1/4 teaspoon hickory seasoned salt

Preheat oven to 400 degrees. Heat the peanut oil over high heat
in a large, heavy skillet. Being sure there is no excess water on the
chops (dry with paper towel if necessary), brown them about a
minute per side in the skillet. Place chops in the bottom of a
baking dish just big enough to hold them in a single layer. Add the
onions and garlic to the drippings in the skillet and cook until the
onions are soft, about five minutes. To this add the tomatoes,
beer, lemon juice, Worcestershire sauce, hickory salt and pepper.
Boil for one minute, remove from heat and pour evenly over the
chops in the baking dish. Place in the oven, uncovered, and bake for
no more than 10 minutes. This should result in the chops being no
more than medium rare which is appropriate.

Sonny's Venison Kabob

Calories: 206   Diabetic Exchanges:
Pro: 29   Lean Meat: 3
Fat: 5   Vegetable: 0
CHO: 14   Bread: 1

1-1 1/2 pounds venison backstrap or other tender cuts
1 pound fresh, whole mushrooms garlic powder
2 large Vidalia onions   fresh ground pepper
2-3 green peppers   2-3 fresh tomatoes

Prepare the marinade by mixing ingredients of Good Seasons
Italian salad dressing in a cruet or following the directions on the
package. Add one teaspoon Italian seasoning to the dressing and
shake well. Cut venison into 2 inch pieces, place in a covered bowl

and mix with half the marinade 24 hours before cooking. Leave in refrigerator and turn meat three or four times during the 24 hours. Thread pieces of meat and vegetables on skewers. Brush or pour the rest of the marinade on the kabobs. Season with fresh ground pepper and garlic power to taste. Cook on grill 10 minutes on each side. Serve with rice pilaf or potatoes. Serves 6-8.

Roast Leg of Venison

Calories: 213

Pro: 29

Fat: 10

CHO: 3

Diabetic Exchanges:

Lean Meat: 4

Vegetable: 0

Bread: 0

6 pound leg of venison

4 cups dry red wine

1 large onion, sliced

1 clove garlic, minced

1 bay leaf

6 peppercorns

4 juniper berries

6 slices of bacon

This recipe can be made with the leg bone left in or removed. Mix the wine, onion, garlic, bay leaf, peppercorns, and juniper berries to make a marinade for the venison. After the meat is added to the marinade it should be refrigerated for 24 hours, turning occasionally so that all parts of the meat are equally marinated. Preheat oven to 450 degrees. Remove the meat from the marinade, drain and strain the marinade and reserve. Place meat in a shallow roasting pan. Put several wraps of meat string around the leg to insure it doesn't fall apart. Lay strips of bacon across the top of the meat and insert a meat thermometer. If bone has been left in the leg, be sure the thermometer is not touching the bone. Roast in the oven for 20 minutes. Reduce the heat to 325 degrees, add the marinade by pouring over the top of the meat and cook until thermometer reaches 140 degrees. This should take about 1 1/2 hours. Baste frequently and check thermometer each time. Do not overcook.

ROASTS & STEAKS

Crockpot Barbecue

Calories: 208
Pro: 36
Fat: 6
CHO: 4

Diabetic Exchanges:
Lean Meat: 4
Vegetable: 0
Bread: 0

3-4 lb venison ham or shoulder
1 large bottle barbecue sauce
Heavy Duty aluminum foil

1 pound bacon
1 small bottle hot
barbecue sauce

Place a large piece of foil in the bottom of a roasting pan. Place meat on the foil. Do not cover meat, but fold the foil partially up the sides of the meat. Drape all the bacon over the top of the meat. In the pan around the outside of the foil pour 2-3 inches of water. The water should not contact the meat only the foil. Place in a preheated oven at 350 degrees and cook for 1 1/2 hours. Remove meat from oven, let cool enough to cut into chunks and put meat into the crock pot. Cover with a combination of barbecue sauces. Cook on low setting overnight or approximately 12-14 hours. Stir periodically. If needed add additional sauce.

Venison Scallopini

Calories: 273
Pro: 35
Fat: 9
CHO: 8

Diabetic Exchanges:
Lean Meat: 4
Vegetable: 0
Bread: 1/2

1 1/2 pounds tenderloin, cut across grain 1/4 inch thick
2 tablespoons soft butter
salt and pepper
1/4 cup flour
2 tablespoons cold butter

3 tablespoons olive oil
1/2 dry red wine
1/2 cup beef stock

Dip each of the pieces of venison in flour, shake off the excess lay them aside on a plate or piece of waxed paper. Chop the cold butter into small pieces and along with the olive oil, melt in a large skillet over moderate heat. Add the meat to the skillet with no one piece touching the other. Put in one layer of meat and cook for 45 seconds, turn, add salt and pepper, cook another 45 seconds and remove immediately from the skillet to a plate. Pour the oil mix from the skillet being careful to leaving any drippings and a very small amount of the oil in the bottom of the skillet. Add the wine and half the stock (1/4 cup) and boil for 1 1/2 minutes. Return the meat to the skillet and simmer on low heat for a couple of minutes using the liquid to baste several times. Remove meat and place on a heated platter. Add the remaining stock and boil until the mixture becomes syrupy. Take skillet off the heat and blend in the soft butter. Pour this sauce over the meat and serve immediately. Serves 6.

Venison De Vinci

Calories: 200
Pro: 36
Fat: 4
CHO: 2

Diabetic Exchanges:
Lean Meat: 4
Vegetable: 0
Bread: 0

1 cup burgundy
2 tablespoons ketchup
2 tablespoons vinegar
1 teaspoon rosemary
1 teaspoon m.s.g.
onions
green pepper

1 cup mazola
1 tablespoon liquid smoke
1 teaspoon marjoram
1 teaspoon salt
1 tablespoon sugar
mushrooms
venison

Marinate venison in all these ingredients for 24 hours. Remove and broil until brown. Do not overcook. Serve with rice.

Venison Bake With Sherry

Calories: 220
Pro: 36
Fat: 6
CHO: 5

Diabetic Exchanges:
Lean Meat: 4
Vegetable: 1
Bread: 0

4 pounds venison (serving sized pieces)
2 cups red wine vinegar
2 large cloves garlic, crushed
2 tablespoons chopped parsley
1 medium sized onion, chopped
4 slices salt pork or bacon
salt and pepper

3 cups white dinner wine
   (Sauterne is good)
2 cloves
3 tablespoons flour
1 cup Sherry

Pour wine vinegar and white wine into a saucepan and bring to a boil. Remove from heat and add garlic, parsley, cloves and onion; cool. Put venison in a glass or porcelain dish and pour the cooled marinade over it. Place in the refrigerator for 10 hours or overnight. Take the meat from the marinade and dry with paper towels. Rub each piece with flour. Put meat in a baking pan and top with slice of salt pork or strips of bacon. Onion slices can be layered on top if desired. Brown in a hot (400 degrees) oven on both sides or about 30 minutes total. Add the cup of marinade, reduce the heat to 350 degrees and roast for about 1 1/2 hours or until tender, adding more marinade if necessary. Pour Sherry over the meat and simmer for about 10 minutes more. Salt and pepper to taste.

Sausage Stuffed Venison

Calories: 296
Pro: 29
Fat: 20
CHO:

Diabetic Exchanges:
Medium Fat Meat: 4
Vegetable: 0
Bread: 0

1 venison tenderloin
bacon

commercial hot (spicy)
sausage

Slice tenderloin lengthways about 2/3 of the way through and lay open. On the inside of the cut place sausage the length of the piece of tenderloin you have. Sausage should be about an inch deep. Wrap bacon slices around the tenderloin, holding in the sausage and pin together with sturdy, round toothpicks. Grill for about 30 minutes. An alternate method is to carefully cut an "X" lengthwise in the interior of the tenderloin and insert a previously frozen 1 inch stick of sausage. The sausage has to be frozen in order to get it to slide into the tenderloin. Place the meat, wrapped in plastic wrap in the refrigerator for a hour or so to give the sausage some time to thaw. Grill about 30 minutes.

Venison Scallopine

Calories: 250
Pro: 36
Fat: 10
CHO: 5

Diabetic Exchanges:
Lean Meat: 4
Vegetable: 1
Bread: 0

2 1/2 pounds venison
1 (4 ounce) can of mushrooms
cooking oil
1 1/4 cup tomato puree

flour seasoned with pepper
   and paprika
2 medium onions, sliced
1 1/4 cup hot water

Cut the venison into serving size pieces, coat with seasoned flour and pound lightly with meat hammer. Brown on both sides in cooking oil. When the meat it turned the first time, add the onions. Place meat in a casserole and add all the remaining ingredients. Bake in a moderate oven (350 degrees) for about 2 hours until tender. Salt to taste. Serves 10.

Venison Stroganoff

Calories: 308
Pro: 38
Fat: 9
CHO: 20

Diabetic Exchanges:
Lean Meat: 4
Vegetable: 1
Bread: 1

3 pounds venison shoulder in one inch strips
4 tablespoon vegetable shortening

2 tablespoons flour	*2 tablespoons salt*
2 cups sliced mushrooms	*1 pint sour cream*
1 teaspoon pepper	*2 tablespoons butter*

Trim meat and cut against the grain into strips 1 inch wide and 1/4 inch thick. Heat shortening in frying pan and cook meat covered until brown. Add one cup of water and steam until strips are tender. Add mushrooms and cook until they begin to wilt. Remove meat and mushrooms from the frying pan and set aside. Add butter and flour to juices left in frying pan and brown. Mix in sour cream and let juices cook slowly together for about five minutes or until they are smooth. Pour this sauce over venison and mushrooms and cook 10 minutes. Serve over flat noodles.

Venison Teriyaki

Calories: 265
Pro: 34
Fat: 9
CHO: 9

Diabetic Exchanges:
Lean Meat: 4
Vegetable: 0
Bread: 1/2

2 pounds venison	*1/4 cup soy sauce*
1 tablespoon brown sugar	*1 tablespoon minced onion*
1 tablespoon wine vinegar	*2 or 3 medium onions, sliced*

2 tablespoons bacon grease
1 teaspoon cornstarch rice or Chinese noodles
1/2 teaspoon powdered or grated ginger root

Trim all fat off meat and cut into thin strips. Combine soy sauce, sugar, minced onion, vinegar and ginger. A dash of garlic powder can be added if desired. Pour over meat and let stand for about two hours. Drain and reserve the marinade. Heat bacon drippings in heavy skillet. Brown meat on all sides. Add onions, cover and cook over low heat for 15 minutes or until meat is tender. Mix cornstarch with reserved marinade and pour over meat and onions. Cook until slightly thickened. Serve over Chinese noodles or rice.

Red Venison Stroganoff

Calories: 306
Pro: 36
Fat: 14
CHO: 8

Diabetic Exchanges:
Lean Meat: 4
Vegetable: 0
Bread: 1

1 1/2 pounds venison
1 can tomato soup
1 tablespoon Worcestershire
1/2 teaspoon salt
1 6-ounce can of mushrooms

flour
2 tablespoons shortening
1 clove garlic, minced
1/2 onion, minced
1 1/2 cups of sour cream

Venison should be cut in about 1 - 1 1/2 inch cubes, dredged in flour and browned in a heavy skillet in which the shortening has been melted. Drain the can of mushrooms and save the liquid. In the skillet with the meat add the onion, garlic and mushrooms. Mix the soup, mushroom liquid and seasonings in a bowl and pour over the meat. Simmer for about 1 hour until tender. At the end of that time and just before serving, stir in the sour cream and heat the entire mixture to serving temperature.

Venison Goulash

Calories: 318
Pro: 37
Fat: 12
CHO: 12

Diabetic Exchanges:
Lean Meat: 4
Vegetable: 0
Bread: 1

3 pounds venison
1/2 cup flour
1 8 ounce can tomato sauce
1 1/2 cups beef broth
1 cup sour cream

1 tablespoon paprika
1 cup dry red wine
1 cup onions, chopped
2 cloves garlic, minced
2 tsp. salt & 4 tbl. butter

Pound the venison pieces lightly with a meat hammer or edge of a small plate, sprinkle with flour and pound it in. Cut into 1 1/2 cubes. Melt butter or margarine in a cast iron skillet and saute onions and garlic for 10 minutes. Add the meat and brown well on all sides. Mix in the salt, paprika, wine, tomato sauce, and broth. Cover and cook over low heat 2 1/2 hours or until meat is tender. Just before serving, stir in the sour cream. Serves 10-12.

"Chicken" Venison Stroganoff

Calories: 424
Pro: 28
Fat: 22
CHO: 25

Diabetic Exchanges:
Medium Fat Meat: 4
Vegetable: 1
Bread: 1

1/4 cup flour
1/4 teaspoon pepper
1/4 cup butter or margarine
1 can undiluted chicken soup
1 pound fresh mushrooms, sliced

1 1/2 teaspoon salt
1 pound venison cut 1/4
    inch thick
1/2 cup water
1 cup sour cream

Combine flour, salt and pepper. Pound seasoned flour into venison. Cut meat into 1 1/2 inches by 1 inch strips. Melt butter or margarine in frying pan. Brown strips turning frequently. Add diced onion, chicken soup, and mushrooms. Cook uncovered over low heat until mixture thickens and meat is tender. (45 minutes to 1 hour). Just before serving, stir in sour cream. Serve over rice. Makes 6 servings.

Italian Grilled Tenderloin

Calories: 162
Pro: 33
Fat: 4
CHO: 0

Diabetic Exchanges:
Lean Meat: 3
Vegetable: 0
Bread: 0

1 12 ounce bottle Italian dressing 1-2 pounds tenderloin

After removing all the silver colored sinews from the outside of the meat, deeply puncture all sides many times with a sharp fork. Put meat in a plastic bag and pour in the Italian dressing. Close bag with as little air as possible left inside. Refrigerate for 24 hours. Remove meat from the refrigerator, allow to come to room temperature, remove from plastic bag and grill whole over charcoal fire. Serves 12

SHED DEER ANTLERS ARE RARELY FOUND IN THE WOODS. SINCE THEY CONTAIN CALCIUM AND PHOSPHORUS THEY ARE EATEN BY SMALL MAMMALS AND RODENTS. OTHER DEER WILL ALSO GNAW ON SHED ANTLERS.

Venison Omelette for Six

Calories: 508
Pro: 45
Fat: 32
CHO: 10

Diabetic Exchanges:
High Fat Meat: 4
Vegetable: 2
Fat: 1

1 cup broccoli florets
3 carrots chopped
1 medium chopped tomato
1/4 cup sliced black olives
12 eggs, lightly beaten
salt
pepper

2 stalks of celery, chopped
8 ounces mushrooms, sliced
1 firm avocado sliced
1/2 stick butter
4 ounces grated sharp
    cheddar cheese
1 pound diced venison
    tenderloin browned

In a large fry pan, melt butter then add (in order) carrots, celery, broccoli, mushrooms, olives. Saute over medium heat until vegetables are heated thoroughly but still crisp. Add venison, cook until done. Salt and pepper to taste. Pour beaten eggs over the mixture, cook without stirring until eggs are nearly done. Stir in tomato and cheese and complete cooking the eggs. Serve with sliced avocado.

Venison Quiche

Calories: 263
Pro: 16
Fat: 15
CHO: 16

Diabetic Exchanges:
Medium Fat Meat: 2
Bread: 1
Fat: 1

1 cup venison tenderloin browned and cut into cubes
1 nine inch pie shell
4 ounces swiss cheese grated
1 cup steamed and chopped asparagus spears

3 eggs
1 cup milk

Brush pie shell with egg white. Bake at 450 degrees for five minutes. Reset oven to 325 degrees. Put venison, cheese and asparagus into the pie shell. Mix eggs and milk and pour over meat mixture. Bake at 325 degrees for one hour. Serves 6-8.

Fried Venison Tenderloin

Calories: 198
Pro: 26
Fat: 6
CHO: 8

Diabetic Exchanges:
Lean Meat: 3
Vegetable: 0
Bread: 1/2

2 pounds deer tenderloin
3 eggs
2 teaspoons salt

2 cups flour
2 cups cooking oil
2 teaspoons pepper

Slice deer tenderloin 1 inch thick; crack eggs in bowl and beat; place 1 inch tenderloin in bowl with eggs. Put flour, salt and pepper in bag and shake to mix. Place 1 inch tenderloin in bag and shake well. In 10 inch skillet put 2 cups cooking oil and set over medium heat. Place 1 inch floured tenderloin in oil; once bottom side is brown, flip over and brown opposite side. Ready to eat once both sides brown; also good cold. Serves 12.

A DEER WILL NOT RUN WHEN IT CAN WALK AND WILL NOT WALK AWAY FROM DANGER IF IT CAN ESCAPE DETECTION BY REMAINING MOTIONLESS.

Straight Forward Tenderloin

Calories: 210

Pro: 35

Fat: 9

CHO: 4

Diabetic Exchanges:

Lean Meat: 4

Vegetable: 0

Bread: 0

1 venison tenderloin

flour

salt

milk

shortening

Slice the tenderloin across the grain and make into small steaks. Put in a pan or dish and cover with milk and marinate for a half hour. Drain meat and dredge each steak in flour. Fry in a little shortening until lightly browned, salt to taste and serve hot. If steaks are no more than 1/2 inch thick, they will only take about 1 minute frying time on each side.

Basic Venison Steaks

Calories: 298

Pro: 35

Fat: 9

CHO: 19

Diabetic Exchanges:

Lean Meat: 4

Vegetable: 0

Bread: 1

venison steaks

fine dry bread crumbs

dry red wine

olive oil

Steaks can be cut from the hams or hind quarter of deer to the desired thickness. Pound them slightly to tenderize. Marinate in wine for several hours, turning them occasionally. Remove from marinade and pat them dry with a paper towel. Coat them lightly with bread crumbs and fry in olive oil. A cooking option is to broil them for approximately 10 minutes at 550 degrees in the oven.

Venison Swiss Steak

Calories: 273
Pro: 36
Fat: 10
CHO: 8

Diabetic Exchanges:
Lean Meat: 4
Vegetable: 0
Bread: 1/2

2 (1 1/2 pound) venison steaks cut in half
flour   butter or margarine
1 (8 ounce) can tomato sauce   2 small bay leaves
salt and pepper
1 package (1 3/8 ounces) dry onion soup mix
2 teaspoons spaghetti sauce seasoning
1 cup dry red wine (Burgundy or similar)

Dredge steaks in flour. Melt butter in a heavy skillet and brown meat over medium heat or 350 degrees in an electric skillet. Add soup mix, spaghetti sauce seasoning, bay leaves, salt and pepper and pour over wine and tomato sauce. Simmer, covered 30 to 45 minutes or until tender. More wine or water can be added if sauce appears too thick.

DEER SWIM WELL, FAST AND FOR LONG DISTANCES. ONE WAS CLOCKED BY A BOAT AT 13 MPH FOR A QUARTER OF A MILE, THEN SLOWING TO 10 MPH WHILE SUCCESSFULLY CROSSING A LARGE LAKE 7 MILES WIDE.

BBQ Steak Casserole

Calories: 292
Pro: 35
Fat: 12
CHO: 9

Diabetic Exchanges:
Lean Meat: 4
Vegetable: 0
Bread: 1

2 pounds venison steaks
1/2 teaspoon pepper
3 tablespoons butter
1 bottle barbecue sauce

1 teaspoon salt
flour
1 large onion, minced
1/2 cup red wine

Prepare steaks in serving size pieces and sprinkle with salt and pepper. Dredge in flour, melt butter in a heavy skillet and brown meat. Multilayer the steaks, onion and barbecue sauce in a casserole. Pour wine over the top and cover. Bake at 350 degrees for 1 hour. White wine can be substituted for a different flavor.

Venison Casserole

Calories: 408
Pro: 32
Fat: 20
CHO: 23

Diabetic Exchanges:
Lean Meat: 4
Vegetable: 1
Bread: 1 Fat: 1

1 pound cabbage, shredded fine
1/2 cup chopped celery
1 chopped onion
1/2 teaspoon salt
1/2 teaspoon crushed fresh pepper corns
1 pound venison steak cut into cubes

1 chopped bell pepper
  (red or green)
1/2 pound pork sausage

Steam cabbage, green pepper, and onion in a little water until wilted. Brown meats in olive oil. Add a little water, cook over low heat until tender, add chopped celery.

In greased casserole dish, alternate layers of meat mixture and cabbage mixture sprinkling with a little flour. Add sliced vegetables of your choice with 1/4 cup of water on top, cover and let steam in 350 degree oven until the top vegetables are done. Serves 8-10.

Venison Pepper Steak

Calories: 271
Pro: 36
Fat: 7
CHO: 14

Diabetic Exchanges:
Lean Meat: 4
Vegetable: 0
Bread: 1

1 1/2 to 2 pounds venison steak
1 small onion, chopped
2-3 tablespoons oil
1/2 cup water
pepper and salt

4 cloves fresh garlic, crushed
1 large onion, sliced
Worcestershire sauce
1 large bell pepper, sliced
4 cups cooked rice

Wash venison and cut into 1/4 inch strips. Heat oil in electric skillet. Quickly brown meat, stirring constantly. Add chopped onion, garlic, 2 tablespoons Worcestershire, 1/2 cup water. Cover with tight-fitting lid, reduce heat to simmer on very low setting for about 20 to 30 minutes, stirring every 10 minutes. Increase heat to medium setting. Add sliced onion, bell pepper and 2 or 3 tablespoons more Worcestershire sauce, salt and pepper. Toss until onion and pepper are tender. Serve over rice. Serves 8.

A WHITETAIL'S TOP SPEED IS **35-40** MPH AND WHEN JUMPING CAN HAVE A SPAN BETWEEN TRACKS OF **29+** FEET.

Smoked Deer Ham

Calories: 215

Pro: 34

Fat: 9

CHO: 0

Diabetic Exchanges:

Lean Meat: 4

Vegetable: 0

Bread: 0

5 pounds deer ham

2 tablespoons brown sugar

1 onion

1 cup zesty Italian dressing

2 tablespoons Worcestershire

Marinate overnight. Remove from marinade. Slice onion and place over deer ham; place deer ham on aluminum foil. Pour excess marinade over deer ham; double wrap deer ham with foil. Cook in smoker approximately 3 hours.

Grilled Steaks With Grilled Roasted Red Potatoes

Calories: 305

Pro: 36

Fat: 9

CHO: 19

Diabetic Exchanges:

Lean Meat: 4

Vegetable: 0

Bread: 1

1 each venison tenderloin steak

1 teaspoon cracked black pepper

2 teaspoons sugar

2 teaspoons vinegar white

4 ounces olive oil

1 teaspoon chopped thyme

1 teaspoons chopped basil

Mix all above ingredients and let marinate overnight. Grill on hot grill until medium rare.

4 red potatoes

1 chopped clove of garlic

3 ounces butter

1 quart seasoned water (salt and pepper)

Wash potatoes, do not peel or cut. Boil in seasoned water until fork tender. Remove from water and hold in refrigerator for at least one hour. Rub with butter and garlic then roast in broiler or grill.

Broiled Venison Steak

Calories: 487

Pro: 35

Fat: 28

CHO: 27

Diabetic Exchanges:

High Fat Meat: 4

Vegetable: 0

Bread: 1

1 venison steak, 3/4 to 1 inch thick

1 cup dry red wine

salt

freshly ground pepper

4 tablespoons butter, melted

1/2 cup currant jelly

1/4 teaspoon allspice

Preheat broiler. Rub venison with butter and sprinkle with salt and pepper. Place the steak 4 inches beneath the broiling element on a rack in a shallow pan. Broil approximately 4 minutes each side. Remove the steak to a warm platter and set the pan over a burner. Add the wine, jelly and allspice to the pan drippings. Bring this mixture to a boil and stir until well blended. Spoon sauce over the steak and serve. Serves 2.

> ## PRONGHORN ANTELOPE WERE ONCE DOWN TO LESS THE 25,000 INDIVIDUALS IN THE WILD; TODAY THERE ARE OVER 1 MILLION.

Venison Salisbury Steaks

Calories: 332

Pro: 26

Fat: 12

CHO: 29

Diabetic Exchanges:

Lean Meat: 3

Vegetable: 0

Bread: 2

1 pound ground venison

1/2 cup milk

1 cup cracker crumbs

dash of pepper

flour

1 egg

1 small onion

1 tablespoon salt

1 cup mushroom soup

oil

Combine meat, egg, milk, onion, cracker crumbs and salt and pepper. Make into patties and roll in flour. Put in hot skillet with small amount of oil and brown. Put in baking pan; cover with cream of mushroom soup. Bake at 350 degrees for 45 minutes. Serves 6.

Venison Roast

Calories: 205

Pro: 36

Fat: 6

CHO: 5

Diabetic Exchanges:

Lean Meat: 4

Vegetable: 0

Bread: 0

5 pounds of deer ham

1 12 ounce can sliced carrots

1 envelope dry onion soup mix

2 1/2 cups water

2 good size potatoes, sliced

1 onion (Vidalia works best)

1/2 cup flour

oven bag

Lightly brown deer ham in skillet; place deer ham in oven bag; sprinkle 1/2 cup flour over deer ham. Add sliced potatoes, carrots, and onion over deer ham. Add 2 1/2 cups water then spread onion soup mix over ham. Seal oven bag and bake 1 1/2 hours on 325 degrees. Salt and pepper to taste.

Venison Pepper Steak

Calories: 295
Pro: 38
Fat: 9
CHO: 14

Diabetic Exchanges:
Lean Meat: 4
Vegetable: 2
Bread: 0

1 pound venison, cut in thin strips
1 dove garlic, minced
1 cup tomatoes
2 teaspoons soy sauce
salt and pepper to taste
2 green peppers, cut in thin strips
1 medium to small onion, cut in rings

2 tablespoons oil
1 cup beef bouillon
1 1/2 tablespoons cornstarch
1/4 cup water

Place oil in skillet. Saute venison, onion and garlic. Add peppers and bouillon; cover and cook about 30 minutes. Add tomatoes and cook 5 more minutes, stirring constantly. Salt and pepper to taste. Serve over rice. Yield: 4 servings.

> IN THE NORTHERN U.S., WHITETAILS HAVE A DISTINCTLY REDDISH COAT IN THE SUMMER MONTHS TURNING TO GREY IN THE AUTUMN. THIS IS MUCH MORE NOTICEABLE IN THE NORTH THAN THE SOUTH.

Deer Steak Marinade

Calories: 225
Pro: 34
Fat: 9
CHO: 1

Diabetic Exchanges:
Lean Meat: 4
Vegetable: 0
Bread: 0

1/2 cup red wine
1 large clove garlic, crushed
3 tablespoons soy sauce

1/2 teaspoon onion powder
1/3 cup olive oil
2 large or 4 small deer steaks

Combine ingredients and pour marinade over deer steaks. Marinate steaks for 2 to 3 hours, turning occasionally. Drain steaks and broil to desired doneness over charcoal. Brush with marinade while steaks are broiling. Yield: 4 servings.

Deer Cube Steak

Calories: 308
Pro: 40
Fat: 8
CHO: 19

Diabetic Exchanges:
Lean Meat: 4
Vegetable: 0
Bread: 1

1 packet deer cube steak
2 eggs
1 cup oil

1 1/2 cup milk
2 cups flour
salt and pepper to taste

Soak deer cube steak 10 minutes in 1 1/2 cup milk. Mix 2 eggs in bowl. Dip cube steak in eggs and sprinkle or dip in flour and salt and pepper. Cook in skillet with 1 cup oil over medium heat until both sides are brown.

> ## THERE ARE **20** MILLION HUNTERS IN THE **U.S.** TODAY.

Venison Roast With Currant Jelly

Calories: 240
Pro: 34
Fat: 9
CHO: 5

Diabetic Exchanges:
Lean Meat: 4
Vegetable: 0
Bread: 1/2

6 pounds venison roast saddle or rib

8 slices of bacon	**3 tablespoons butter**
3 tablespoons flour	**2 teaspoons salt**
1/4 teaspoon pepper	**1 cup red currant jelly**
3 tablespoons flour	**2 cups hot milk**
1/2 cup light cream	

While preheating oven to 375 degrees, rub venison with salt, pepper and then lay the bacon slices across the top of the meat. Place in roasting pan and cook in the oven for 30 minutes. Take from oven but keep the meat warm. Turn oven down to 325 degrees. Melt the butter in a saucepan, blend in the flour, add the milk while constantly stirring and bring to just below the boiling point. Add the roasting pan drippings and cook over a low heat for about 5 minutes. Pour the sauce over the roast and return to the oven to cook for about 1 1/2 hours or until tender, basting frequently. When meat is cooked to medium rare, remove from the pan and place on the serving platter. Pour the gravy back into a saucepan and skim the fat off the top. Stir the jelly into the gravy first and then the cream. Cook for five minutes. Serve the sauce in a bowl of its own beside the platter of venison.

THE SIZE OF A DEER'S ANTLERS IS A FUNCTION OF NUTRITION AND NOT AGE.

Brandy Roast Tenderloin

Calories: 210
Pro: 35
Fat: 4
CHO: 6

Diabetic Exchanges:
Lean Meat: 4
Vegetable: 0
Bread: 0

2 pounds tenderloin
1 whole clove
3 parsley sprigs
1/2 teaspoon salt
2 tablespoons butter
1 small bay leaf
1/2 cup chicken stock
1/2 cup red wine
1/2 cup water
1/8 teaspoon thyme
ground pepper
1 tablespoon oil
2 tablespoons flour
2 tablespoons brandy
1 medium onion, cut into 1/8 inch slices
2 tablespoons finely chopped shallots or scallions

In a small bowl, combine the red wine, water, sliced onion, shallots, cinnamon, bay leaf, clove, parsley, thyme, salt and several twists of the pepper grinder. Cut the tenderloin across the grain into 1/4 inch thick slices, and arrange them in a single layer in a shallow baking dish. Pour the marinade over them, turning them several times to insure each slice is well soaked. Set aside without refrigeration for 2-4 hours, turning each piece several times. Preheat oven to 300 degrees. Remove venison pieces from the liquid and pat dry with a paper towel. Retain the entire marinade. Put butter (or margarine) and oil in a heavy skillet and melt over low heat. Evenly brown each venison slice and transfer to a shallow baking dish. Arrange slices in a single layer, touching but not overlapping. Strain the marinade through a fine sieve, pressing the solids against the sides with enough force to extract the juices but not forcing any material through into the liquid. Do not save the remaining solids. Add the flour to the hot skillet and cook until it turns lightly brown. Slowly pour in the strained marinade, brandy and chicken stock.

While stirring constantly, bring to a boil and cook until the mixture is slightly thickened. Pour the mixture over the venison slices in the baking dish. Put into preheated oven and bake for about 10 - 12 minutes, basting with the sauce in the bottom of the dish.

Buck in a Bag

Calories: 195
Pro: 35
Fat: 4
CHO: 3

Diabetic Exchanges:
Lean Meat: 4
Vegetable: 0
Bread: 0

1/4 cup flour
1 cup dry red wine
1 cup water
4 pound venison roast
12 juniper berries
1/2 teaspoon thyme

2 tablespoons dried basil
1 large onion, chopped
1 bay leaf
2 cloves garlic, chopped
salt and pepper

Preheat oven to 350 degrees. In the bottom of a small cooking bag placed in the bottom of a roasting pan, pour the flour. Add the wine and the water, slowly mixing it until it is thoroughly blended. Lightly salt and pepper the roast and place in the bag. Add the rest of the ingredients inside the bag and close according to bag directions. Several cuts need to be made in the bag to allow steam to escape while cooking. This amount of roast should take about 2 hours to cook. After the roast is finished and removed, the juices in the bag can be made into gravy.

> ## OF ALL THE DEER FAMILY, THE WHITETAIL IS FOUND IN THE GREATEST VARIETY OF HABITAT.

Pit Roasted Venison

Calories: 180

Pro: 34

Fat: 4

CHO: 0

Diabetic Exchanges:

Lean Meat: 4

Vegetable: 0

Bread: 0

Keep a good fire going in a pit about 1 foot deep until it is full of red coals. Have at least 4 to 6 inches of red coals for your roasting pit. Prepare a roast of venison with salt, pepper and any other seasoning you desire. Place in three separate layers of heavy foil and seal edges by carefully folding them together. Bank coals around roast 6 to 8 hours. Remove coals carefully, remove first and second layer of foil to insure the third layer is clean. Use care opening the final layer of foil. Save the juices to serve over the sliced roast meat.

Pot Roast in Barbecue Sauce

Calories: 193

Pro: 35

Fat: 4

CHO: 2

Diabetic Exchanges:

Lean Meat: 4

Vegetable: 0

Bread: 0

4 pounds rump, round or chuck venison

1 cup tomato sauce

1/2 cup vinegar

1/4 teaspoon pepper

1/4 teaspoon paprika

3 teaspoons salt

2 teaspoons chili powder

Brown meat thoroughly on all sides in a heavy kettle or Dutch oven. Mix together the tomato sauce, vinegar, salt, pepper, chili powder and paprika. Pour over browned meat. Cover and simmer gently over low heat, until tender. Turn meat several times during cooking and add a little water if necessary to keep meat from sticking.

For a thicker gravy, remove meat to a serving platter, mix 1 tablespoon flour and 2 tablespoons water to a smooth paste, and stir into the liquid in the kettle. Simmer a couple of minutes to cook the flour.

Barbecued Venison

Cut 1 1-1/2 pounds venison stew meat in cubes about 1 1/2 inch to 2 inch squares and brown in medium-hot oil. While venison is browning in a heavy skillet, make sauce as follows:

Calories: 230
Pro: 36
Fat: 7
CHO: 5

Diabetic Exchanges:
Lean Meat: 4
Vegetable: 1
Bread: 0

1/2 cup ketchup
2 tablespoons brown sugar
1/2 teaspoon black pepper
Juice of 1/2 lemon

1/2 cup wine vinegar
1 teaspoon salt
1/2 tablespoon cayenne
pepper

Place ingredients in a saucepan and simmer for 20 minutes. Add venison and stir to cover all pieces well. In separate saucepan fry one medium sweet onion. Add cooked onions to venison, cook covered until tender. Watch to be sure the sauce does not cook dry, and add more liquid if necessary. Serve with your choice of vegetable side dishes.

The Easiest Roast

Calories: 190
Pro: 35
Fat: 4
CHO: 3
**1/2 envelope of dry
onion soup mix**

Diabetic Exchanges:
Lean Meat: 4
Vegetable: 0
Bread: 0
4 pound venison roast

Preheat oven to 425 degrees. Using the heavy duty aluminum foil, place roast in the center of a large sheet and cover with the dry onion soup mix. All that remains is to be sure that the foil is folded over and sealed tightly. Place the foil package in the bottom of a roasting pan and cook for about 2+ hours.

Smothered Steak

Calories: 260
Pro: 36
Fat: 9
CHO: 7
2 pounds venison steaks
1/4 cup green peppers, chopped
1 teaspoon salt
1 teaspoon celery salt
1/4 teaspoon pepper
2 tablespoons peanut oil

Diabetic Exchanges:
Lean Meat: 4
Vegetable: 1
Bread: 0
2 onions, sliced
1/4 cup all-purpose flour
2 1/3 cups tomatoes
   (1 pound, 3 ounce can)
Louisiana hot pepper sauce

In a cast iron skillet, heat the oil. Prepare the seasoned flour by adding the salt, celery salt and pepper. Dredge meat in flour mixture and put in skillet. Brown the steaks well on both sides. Over the meat add the tomatoes, onion and green pepper. Add a couple dashes of hot sauce. Place in preheated oven at 300 degrees for two hours or until the meat is tender. Serves 6-8.

Venison Pot Roast

Calories: 279
Pro: 42
Fat: 5
CHO: 16

Diabetic Exchanges:
Lean Meat: 4
Vegetable: 0
Bread: 1/2

3 pounds venison roast
3 medium onions, chopped
6 cloves garlic, minced
2 teaspoons black pepper
1/2 teaspoon red pepper
2 teaspoons salt

6 cups buttermilk
1 cup water
1 can onion soup
2/3 cup Port wine (or sherry)
1/2 pound mushrooms, sliced
2 tablespoons cooking oil

Place garlic, onions, peppers and salt in a small bowl and mix well. Cut several small slits into the meat and stuff mixture into the holes deep enough that the meat closes back over the mixture. Save enough mixture to rub on the outside of the roast. Place the roast in a deep bowl and add buttermilk. Cover bowl tightly with plastic wrap and refrigerate. Allow roast to marinate for at least 4 hours. Remove roast from milk and pat dry with paper toweling. In a deep, heavy skillet, heat the oil and brown the roast on all sides. Add onion soup and water to skillet and cook for 2 to 3 hours, covered, on medium low heat. 1/2 hour before roast is done, add mushrooms and wine. The liquid and drippings left in the skillet may be thickened with a flour and water mixture for gravy. Serves 12.

USING ONLY THEIR SENSE OF SMELL, DEER CAN LOCATE FOOD SUCH AS APPLES, ACORNS AND CORN UNDER A FOOT OF FRESHLY FALLEN SNOW.

Country Fried Steak With Pan Gravy

Calories: 293

Pro: 37

Fat: 11

CHO: 15

Diabetic Exchanges:

Lean Meat: 4

Vegetable: 0

Bread: 1

1 pound venison steak

1/2 teaspoon garlic powder

1/4 teaspoon Worcestershire sauce

6 tablespoons shortening or oil

4 tablespoons flour

salt and pepper

2 cups milk

Pound steak with a meat hammer until thin. Wipe steak with a damp paper towel and roll in flour, coating both sides. Slowly heat large, heavy skillet. Add shortening. When hot, add steak and brown well on both sides, turning with tongs for approximately 8 to 10 minutes of cooking time. Remove meat and place on a hot platter. To make the gravy, take 3 tablespoons of oil from the skillet being sure to scrape and include all possible drippings and place in a saucepan. Add 4 tablespoons flour and garlic powder and mix well. Slowly stir in the milk. Cook on medium low heat until thickened, stirring constantly. Add salt, pepper and Worcestershire sauce. Spoon onto steak or serve gravy separately. Good served with mashed or fried potatoes and turnip greens. Serves 4.

Hunters Barbecue Venison

Calories: 306

Pro: 36

Fat: 4

CHO: 25

Diabetic Exchanges:

Lean Meat: 4

Vegetable: 0

Bread: 1

2 pounds venison, 2 inch cubes 	8 red new whole potatoes,
 sliced in half 	1 medium onion, sliced
2 cups of your favorite barbecue sauce
1 teaspoon lemon pepper

Mix all the ingredients in a crockpot and cook for 8 hours on the low setting. Stir several times. After 8 hours pour off all the liquid (including the barbecue sauce) and add a fresh cup of barbecue sauce and cook for 8 hours more. Serve in bowls. Serves 8.

Baked Hash Southern Style

Calories: 270

Pro: 41

Fat: 5

CHO: 16

Diabetic Exchanges:

Lean Meat: 3

Vegetable: 1

Bread: 1

3 cups venison, cooked leftovers, diced
1 1/2 teaspoons salt
2 cups diced raw potatoes
1 1/2 cups onion, chopped
1/2 cup red bell peppers, chopped
1/4 cup green peppers, chopped
1 teaspoon Worcestershire sauce
1 dash Tabasco sauce
1/2 teaspoon black pepper
1/4 teaspoon thyme
1 10 1/2 ounce can
 beef gravy
3 tablespoons minced parsley

Mix all ingredients together and place in a greased 2 quart casserole. Cover and bake in a 375 degree oven for 1 hour. Remove the cover for the last 15 minutes of cooking. Serves 12.

IF YOU THINK YOU'RE A GOOD STALKER OR TRACKER, READ TOM BROWN, JR'S BOOK, THE TRACKER.

Broiled African Style Steak

Calories: 193
Pro: 32
Fat: 6
CHO: 2

Diabetic Exchanges:
Lean Meat: 4
Vegetable: 0
Bread: 0

2 each 1 pound venison steaks
1 teaspoon salt
2 tablespoons Worcestershire sauce
1/2 teaspoon black pepper

1/2 teaspoon sage
4 tablespoons butter

Mix salt, pepper and sage and rub by hand on both sides of each steak. Place in a greased pan and put under the oven broiler. Broil about 6-8 minutes per side for a 1 inch thick steak. Melt the butter, add to the Worcestershire sauce and brush the surface of the steaks several times during cooking.

Rily's Venison Pot Roast

Calories: 260
Pro: 35
Fat: 11
CHO: 6

Diabetic Exchanges:
Lean Meat: 4
Vegetable: 0
Bread: 1/2

1 venison roast (2-3 pounds)
1 envelope of dry onion soup mix
1 can of cream of mushroom soup

1/2 cup cooking oil
3 cans of water

In a deep, heavy skillet heat cooking oil and brown roast on all sides over medium heat. Add dry and canned soup and 3 cans of water over the roast. Cover and simmer until meat is very tender, approximately 1 - 1 1/2 hours. Serve over rice.

Steak Au Poivre

Calories: 180

Pro: 23

Fat: 8

CHO: 3

Diabetic Exchanges:

Lean Meat: 3

Vegetable: 0

Bread: 0

8 venison tenderloin steaks, 1 inch thick

4 tablespoons black peppercorns, coarsely crushed

2 tablespoons unsalted butter, cold, finely chopped

3 tablespoons butter   1/4 cup Cognac

1 1/2 cups beef stock

After cutting the steaks across the grain, pat dry with paper towels and sprinkle each side of each steak with crushed pepper. Push the pepper into the steak with the back of a spoon or your fingers. Set aside. Heat the butter in a large, heavy skillet. Place the steaks in the pan and saute for about 1 1/2 minutes, turn them over, salt them lightly and saute the other side for the same period of time. Remove steaks from the skillet and place them on a heated serving platter. Into the still hot skillet, gently and carefully pour the cognac. This mixture should flame up. If not, light it with a match to burn off the alcohol. When flame has gone out, add the stock. Stir while scraping the bottom of the skillet to get the drippings into the mix. Bring to a boil for just a minute. Remove from heat, pass the mixture through a fine strainer into another saucepan and reheat. Remove from heat again and add the chopped butter to the sauce in the pan and beat with a whisk to blend. Pour sauce over the steaks on the platter, add some green garnish such as parsley and serve at once.

Venison Hash

Calories: 410
Pro: 40
Fat: 12
CHO: 35

Diabetic Exchanges:
Lean Meat: 4
Vegetable: 1
Bread: 2

4 pounds leftover (already cooked) venison roast, chopped
4 tablespoons flour
2 tablespoons peanut oil
1 cup beef stock
1/4 teaspoon black pepper
2 pounds raw potatoes, chopped
1 pound mushrooms, chopped
1/8 teaspoon sage
1/2 teaspoon garlic powder
1/2 teaspoon black pepper

In a cold saucepan, combine the peanut oil and flour. Blend thoroughly with a whisk. Gradually add the beef stock and blend well with oil and flour mixture. Cook over medium heat until the mixture is thickened and add pepper. Set this sauce aside. In a large saucepan place the venison and potatoes and cover with the sauce previously made. Simmer uncovered for about 20 minutes and then add the mushrooms. Simmer for an additional 10 minutes. Add the sage, garlic powder and pepper. Mix thoroughly and leave on very low heat for about five minutes. This hash is traditionally served over biscuits or toast often with a fried egg on top. Serves 20.

WHEN DEER WALK STEADILY AT THEIR NORMAL PACE, THEY COVER 3 1/2 - 4 MILES PER HOUR. A LITTLE FASTER THAN A MAN.

Broiled Butterfly Venison Steaks

Calories: 185

Pro: 28

Fat: 9

CHO: 0

Diabetic Exchanges:

Lean Meat: 3

Vegetable: 0

Bread: 0

6 butterflied steaks from the tenderloin

1/8 cup red wine vinegar

1/4 cup olive oil

dash of salt

1/4 teaspoon pepper

1/2 teaspoon oregano

Cut tenderloin across the grain about 1 inch thick. Lay each piece flat on a cutting board, cut about 3/4 of the way through the meat, crossgrain, and lay it open like a book. To make the marinade, mix olive oil, wine vinegar, salt, pepper and oregano together and blend well. Place meat in a shallow dish with each piece laid open and pour the marinade over the meat. Turn the meat several times. Marinate for about 30 minutes. Remove from the marinade, arrange steaks in the open position on heavy aluminum foil and broil in the oven until they are done to your taste. Do not over cook. A few minutes on each side should be satisfactory. Serves 6.

A DEER'S VISION IS GEARED TOWARD MOTION, THE SLIGHTEST MOTION. MOTIONLESS OBJECTS ARE SELDOM SEEN OR RECOGNIZED, NO MATTER THEIR SIZE, SHAPE OR COLOR.

Chinese Skewered Venison

Calories: 210
Pro: 35
Fat: 4
CHO: 8

Diabetic Exchanges:
Lean Meat: 3
Vegetable: 0
Bread: 1/2

1-1/4 pound venison flank steak
1 tablespoon fresh ginger, minced
1/3 cup sugar
2 tablespoons corn starch
1 1/2 tablespoons hoisin (chinese) sauce

1 tablespoon garlic, minced
1/3 cup soy sauce
3-4 cups peanut oil
24-30 wooden skewers

Slice flank steak cross grain 1/8 inch think. Mix all other ingredients except oil to make marinade. Place meat in a shallow container and pour marinade to completely cover. Seal or plastic wrap the container and refrigerator overnight or longer. Remove meat from liquid .and thread onto skewers. Heat peanut oil in a wok until hot enough to deep fry. Drop meat on the skewers into the oil several at a time, turning once, cooking for 20 seconds. Serve hot. Serves 6.

Venison Swiss Steak and Sour Cream

Calories: 374
Pro: 36
Fat: 22
CHO: 8

Diabetic Exchanges:
High Fat Meat: 3
Vegetable: 0
Skim Milk: 1/2

3 pounds venison steaks, 1 inch thick
1/2 cup flour
pepper

salt
2 onions, sliced

1/2 cup water

8 ounces sour cream

4 ounces grated swiss cheese

Flour steaks on both sides, season with salt and pepper. Brown both sides in skillet in hot oil. Add sliced onions. Combine sour cream, cheese, and water and pour over meat. Cover pan and simmer until meat is tender, approximately 2 hours.

Venison Stroganoff

Calories: 346

Diabetic Exchanges:

Pro: 36

Lean Meat: 4

Fat: 19

Vegetable: 1

CHO: 7

Fat: 2

3 pounds venison shoulder in one inch strips

4 tablespoons vegetable shortening

2 tablespoons flour

2 tablespoons salt

2 cups mushrooms, sliced

1 pint sour cream

1 teaspoon pepper

2 tablespoons butter

Trim meat and cut against the grain into strips 1" wide and 1/4" thick. Heat shortening in frying pan and cook meat covered until brown. Add one cup of water and steam until strips are tender. Add mushrooms and cook until they begin to wilt. Remove meat and mushrooms from the frying pan and set aside. Add butter and flour to juices left in frying pan and brown. Mix in sour cream and let all these juices cook slowly together for about five minutes or until they are smooth. Return meat and mushrooms to the frying pan, mix with sauce, and cook 10 minutes. Serve over flat noodles.

> ### THERE IS SUCH A THING AS A DOE WITH ANTLERS, ALTHOUGH IT IS RARE.

Venison Casserole

Calories: 275

Pro: 38

Fat: 13

CHO: 5

Diabetic Exchanges:

Lean Meat: 4

Vegetable: 1

Bread: 0

1 bell pepper (red or green), chopped
1 pound venison steak cut into cubes   1/2 teaspoon salt
1 pound cabbage, shredded fine   1 onion, chopped
1/2 pound pork sausage   1/2 cup celery, chopped
1/2 teaspoon fresh peppercorns, crushed

Steam cabbage, green pepper, and onion in a little water until wilted and set aside. Brown meats in olive oil. Add a little water, cook over low heat until tender, add chopped celery. In greased casserole dish, alternate layers of meat mixture and cabbage, pepper and onions sprinkling with a little flour. Add sliced vegetables of your choice such as carrots or potatoes with 1/4 cup of water on top, cover and let steam in 350 degree oven until the top vegetables are done. Serves 6.

Venison Pot Roast in Barbecue Sauce

Calories: 225

Pro: 36

Fat: 4

CHO: 9

Diabetic Exchanges:

Lean Meat: 3

Vegetable: 0

Bread: 1/2

4 pound rump, round or chuck venison   1 cup tomato sauce
1/2 cup vinegar   3 teaspoons salt

1/4 teaspoon pepper

2 teaspoons chili powder

1/4 teaspoon paprika

Brown meat thoroughly on all sides in a heavy kettle or Dutch oven. Mix together the tomato sauce, vinegar, salt, pepper, chili powder and paprika. Pour over browned meat. Cover and simmer gently over low heat, until tender. Turn meat several times during cooking and add a little water if necessary to keep meat from sticking. For a thicker gravy, remove meat to a serving platter, mix 1 tablespoon flour and 2 tablespoons water to a smooth paste, and stir into the liquid in the kettle.

Special Process Baked Venison

Calories: 199

Pro: 34

Fat: 5

CHO: 1

Diabetic Exchanges:

Lean Meat: 4

Vegetable: 0

Bread: 0

2 pounds venison, loin, ham or shoulder

corn oil

2 cups Bisquick

salt

garlic salt

7-Up (carbonated soft drink)

bay leaves

pepper

Cast iron cooker with a lid that can be put in the oven

Put 2 cups of Bisquick into a plastic bag. Cut venison in thin 1/4 to 1/2 inch slices and drop into the bag about 1/2 pound at a time. Shake to coat venison, remove from bag, retaining a light to medium coating. Lay meat out on a platter and lightly sprinkle with salt and garlic salt. Pepper at the same time, but use a little more than usual. Continue process until all the meat is coated. Pour about 1/4 inch of corn oil in cooker and heat. Slowly brown the meat several pieces at a time for about 4 - 5 minutes. Only brown the meat one layer at a time, remove from cooker and lay on a platter to drain. When all meat is browned, skim off excess oil and leave remaining drippings in the cooker. Return the meat to the cooker, a single layer at a time. Between each layer a bay leaf may be added. Gently add 7-Up, poured around the edges so as not to wash off the Bisquick and seasonings. When all layers have been added, the 7-Up should be about 2/3 the depth of the meat in the cooker. This is a steaming and not a boiling process. Cover the cooker and place in the oven at 350 degrees approximately 1 hour or until tender. Check the level of the liquid from time to time and add more 7-Up if necessary. After the meat is removed for serving, skim and discard any fat from the top of the liquid left in the cooker and it can be used as a delicious gravy.

STEWS, SOUPS, & ORGANS

Parsley Venison With Dumplings

Calories: 275

Pro: 39

Fat: 4

CHO: 18

Diabetic Exchanges:

Lean Meat: 4

Vegetable: 0

Bread: 1

2 pounds venison, cubed stew meat
1/2 cup chopped parsley
1/4 teaspoon pepper

2 onions, chopped
1/2 teaspoon salt
Dumplings

Place venison, onion, and parsley in a deep, cast iron skillet or Dutch oven. Add water to cover the mixture. Cover the skillet and let simmer for 1 to 1 1/2 hours or until the venison is tender. Make Bisquick dumplings according to directions on package and spoon on top of the meat. Maintain heat to keep mixture simmering. Dumplings are cooked for 20 minutes, 10 minutes uncovered and 10 minutes covered. When finished, serve immediately. Serves 8.

Rosemary Venison Chili

Calories: 181

Pro: 26

Fat: 3

CHO: 10

Diabetic Exchanges:

Lean Meat: 3

Vegetable: 0

Bread: 1/2

2 pounds venison, diced
1/4 cup celery, diced
1 tablespoon rosemary, chopped
1 tablespoon dark chili powder
1 1/2 gallons beef stock or bouillon

1/2 cup yellow onion, diced
pepper
2 cups cooked red beans
3 cups tomato, diced
salt

Sear meat and add vegetables. Add chopped rosemary and tomatoes. Add red beans and stock and let reduce 1/4 of the way. Add chili powder, salt and pepper to taste and adjust consistency by reducing until thick. Serves 12.

Venison Stew

Calories: 199	Diabetic Exchanges:
Pro: 25	Lean Meat: 3
Fat: 3	Vegetable: 1
CHO: 18	Bread: 1
1 pound venison	*4 medium potatoes*
1 medium onion	*3-4 carrots*
3-4 celery stalks	*1 cup beef broth*
2-3 cups water	*salt and pepper to taste*

Cut venison into small bite size cubes and place in a hot skillet until brown. Place venison celery and water in kettle. Bring to a boil and cook approximately 1 hour or until meat is tender, adding water if necessary to keep meat covered. Add vegetables to broth. Simmer 15-20 minutes or until vegetables are cooked. Serves 6.

LOW HUMIDITY (10-20%) TENDS TO DRY OUT THE NASAL PASSAGES OF DEER AND SOMEWHAT DEADENS THEIR SENSE OF SMELL. ON HIGH HUMIDITY DAYS, THEY PICK UP SCENTS MUCH BETTER.

Wild Chili

Calories: 163
Pro: 25
Fat: 3
CHO: 8

Diabetic Exchanges:
Lean Meat: 3
Vegetable: 0
Bread: 1/2

2 pounds ground venison
2 tablespoons green pepper
1/2 dry onion soup mix
1 large tomato, chopped
1 1/2 cups kidney beans

1 medium onion
2 cloves garlic
2 1/2 tablespoons chili powder
1 1/2 cups tomato sauce

In 2 tablespoons of cooking oil, brown venison, onion and pepper in large pot. Add remaining ingredients. Cover and simmer 1-2 hours. Serves 10-12.

Easy Venison Stew

Calories: 168
Pro: 25
Fat: 3
CHO: 10

Diabetic Exchanges:
Lean Meat: 3
Vegetable: 2
Bread: 0

1 pound ground venison
1 medium onion
1 1/2 cup water

1 cup vegetable soup
1 large cup mixed vegetables
salt and pepper to taste

Brown ground venison in pot, drain and add remaining ingredients. Cover and cook slowly for 1 hour. Serve with cornbread or crackers. Serves 4-6.

THE WORLD'S SMALLEST DEER IS THE PUDU OF THE ANDES, WHICH STANDS 12 INCHES TALL AND WEIGHS 15 POUNDS.

Fireside Venison Soup

Calories: 264

Pro: 29

Fat: 12

CHO: 8

Diabetic Exchanges:

Lean Meat: 4

Vegetable: 0

Bread: 1/2

1 medium onion finely chopped

1 tablespoon ketchup

3 10 3/4-ounce cans vegetable soup

1 pound ground venison

1/2 cup water

1/2 pound cheese

Brown ground venison and onion. Combine all ingredients, except cheese, in saucepan. Cook 15 minutes and add chunks of your favorite cheese. Cook an additional 5 minutes and serve.

Quick, But Good, Venison Stew

Calories: 193

Pro: 28

Fat: 7

CHO: 4

Diabetic Exchanges:

Lean Meat: 3

Vegetable: 1

Bread: 0

1 - 1 1/2 pounds venison

2 green peppers

1/2 teaspoon pepper

2 medium tomatoes, pealed and quartered

1 (10 3/4 ounce) can beef gravy

2 tablespoons olive oil

1 teaspoon garlic salt

3 tablespoons red wine

Cut meat 1/4 inch thick and into 1 1/2 in squares. Heat Dutch oven over high heat. Add oil, coating sides and bottom of pan; pour out excess. Add venison, peppers, garlic salt and pepper. Stir rapidly and constantly for about 5 minutes. Add wine; continue stirring until wine is blended, about 5 minutes. Reduce heat to simmer. Add tomatoes and beef gravy. Cover tightly and simmer for 10 minutes. Serve immediately. Serves 6-8.

Burgundy Venison Stew

Calories: 236
Pro: 28
Fat: 13
CHO: 2

Diabetic Exchanges:
Lean Meat: 4
Vegetable: 0
Bread: 0

1 1/2 pounds venison, cubed
1/2 teaspoon salt
1/2 teaspoon garlic salt
1/4 cup of butter or margarine
1 onion, chopped
4 sprigs parsley
1 1/2 cups Burgundy (or other red table wine)

2 tablespoons flour
1/2 teaspoon pepper
1/4 cup of oil
2 stalks celery, chopped
2 cloves garlic, chopped
1/2 cup water

Dredge venison in flour seasoned with salt, pepper and garlic salt. In a large heavy skillet, brown the meat in oil and butter. Add the celery and onion and brown well. Add garlic and parsley and brown slightly. Pour water and wine over the meat. Simmer, covered, over low heat or in moderate, slow oven (325 degrees) for 1 to 1 1/2 hours or until tender. Serves 8-10.

Really Easy Chili (Soup)

Calories: 291
Pro: 29
Fat: 7
CHO: 24

Diabetic Exchanges:
Lean Meat: 3
Vegetable: 1
Bread: 1

1 1/2 pound ground venison
2-3 tablespoons chili powder
1 1/2 cup water
salt and pepper

1 large onion, chopped
1 small chili pepper
2 tablespoons cooking oil

1 green bell pepper, cleaned out and chopped
2 16 ounce cans red kidney beans or hot chili beans
2 14.5 ounce cans stewed tomatoes
1 10 3/4 ounce can of condensed tomato soup

In a hot dutch oven type pot pour the oil and add the green pepper. Let cook for a couple minutes, add the onions and cook for another couple a minutes. Sprinkle chili powder over frying mixture and add salt and pepper to taste. Add the ground venison and cook until browned. Do not drain oil away from the meat. Add the beans and tomatoes, undrained. Next add the tomato soup and water. Let simmer for about 20 minutes. Taste and add more chili powder if needed. This will serve 8-10 people depending on how many crackers they eat with it. If you need to stretch it further, add another can of stewed tomatoes.

Split Pea Soup

Calories: 150

Pro: 18

Fat: 2

CHO: 15

Diabetic Exchanges:

Lean Meat: 2

Vegetable: 0

Bread: 1

2 pounds venison, lower ribs, flank meat and bones

3 quarts water

1 tablespoon salt

2 cups split peas, drained

1/2 teaspoon black pepper

2 carrots, grated

2 onions, diced

In a large saucepan place water and peas. Bring to a boil and cook over low heat for 1 hour. Add the entire ribs, salt, pepper, carrots, and onions. Cover and cook over low heat 2 additional hours or until the meat is tender. Remove the meat and bones and run through a sieve. Return soup to a saucepan and reheat. Some of the meat may be cut into small pieces and put back in the soup. Yield is approximately 2 quarts of soup. Serves 16.

Mulligan Stew

Calories: 460
Pro: 64
Fat: 12
CHO: 23

Diabetic Exchanges:
Lean Meat: 6
Vegetable: 2
Bread: 1

2 - 2 1/2 pounds venison roast
3/4 cup red wine vinegar
1/4 cup olive oil
4 juniper berries
1 medium onion
2 cups fresh green beans, sliced
8 peppercorns
1 1/2 cups of canned tomatoes

1/4 cup butter or margarine
1 cup yellow turnips, diced
3/4 cup onions, diced
4 carrots, sliced crosswise
1 cup kernel corn
8 whole cloves
1/2 cup celery, sliced

Prepare a marinade of the vinegar, oil, juniper berries, onion, cloves and peppercorns. Pour into a shallow dish, add meat and seal with plastic wrap. Marinate for 24 hours, turning several times. Remove from marinade, pat dry with paper toweling and cut into approximately 3/4 inch cubes. In a hot skillet melt butter and brown meat on all sides. Cover meat with cold water and bring to a boil. Reduce heat, cover and simmer for 1 1/2 to 2 hours or until meat is tender. All other ingredients are to be added at this time which may necessitate transferring the entire contents of the skillet into a larger pot. Do so if necessary and add all remaining ingredients. Simmer, covered, until the vegetables are tender. Serves 4-6.

Wild Rice and Venison Stew

Calories: 315
Pro: 36
Fat: 10
CHO: 17

Diabetic Exchanges:
Lean Meat: 4
Vegetable: 0
Bread: 1

3 pounds venison, cut into chunks
2 medium onions, quartered
6 cups hot water
2 cups beef stock
3 tablespoons olive oil
1/4 teaspoon garlic powder
1 1/2 cups wild rice
1 bay leaf

In a large skillet, heat the oil, add the meat chunks several pieces at a time and brown lightly. Put venison in a deep stew pot and add water, stock and onions. Leave pot uncovered and simmer slowly for approximately 2 1/2 hours. Add garlic powder, bay leaf and wild rice. Simmer covered for another 20 minutes. Remove the cover, stir well and simmer, uncovered, for another 5 minutes. Serves 12.

Deer Stew

Calories: 267
Pro: 27
Fat: 5
CHO: 24

Diabetic Exchanges:
High Fat Meat: 3
Vegetable: 1
Bread: 1

1 pound Ground Deer meat
1 12 ounce can butter peas
salt & pepper to taste
2 8 ounce cans stewed tomatoes
1 8 ounce can corn
2 cups water

Brown ground deer meat in skillet and drain excess oil. Mix all ingredients in large pot and cook 2 hours over medium heat stirring occasionally. Serves 6.

AN AVERAGE SIZE WHITETAIL HAS ABOUT 6,211,200 HAIRS (5,176 PER SQUARE INCH) IN THE SUMMER MONTHS.

Brains And Eggs

Calories: 451
Pro: 34
Fat: 35
CHO: 0

Diabetic Exchanges:
High Fat Meat: 5
Vegetable: 0
Bread: 0

This recipe is actually for one person as it only uses one brain which is not too large. Brains can be frozen, so you might want to accumulate a couple or so before making this particular recipe. It may not take a long time to get more than one. You'd be surprised how many people would be glad to give you the one from their deer. Don't tell them what they are missing.

1 deer brain (both halves)
2 tablespoons butter or margarine
1/4 teaspoon basil
(or 1/2 teaspoon Italian seasoning instead of basil and thyme)
1/2 teaspoon garlic powder

2 tablespoons vinegar
1 1/2 pint cold water
1/4 teaspoon thyme

2 large eggs

Under cold water, wash the brain well and check to be sure there are no bone fragments or anything else hard adhering to any part. Put the vinegar in the cold water and let the brain soak for about 20 minutes or so. Remove and pat dry. On a cutting board, dice the brain into small pieces. It will be little hard to hold and won't cut very evenly, but that's all right. In a skillet, add the butter or margarine and over medium low heat saute the brain, adding the spices, until it is golden brown, but not hard cooked. Crack the eggs in a separate bowl and beat together. Pour over the meat in the skillet, mix together with a spatula and cook to desired scrambled egg consistency.

Fried Liver

Calories: 238
Pro: 25
Fat: 10
CHO: 9

Diabetic Exchanges:
Lean Meat: 3
Vegetable: 0
Bread: 1

1 pound venison liver
1/2 teaspoon salt
1/4 teaspoon pepper

1 teaspoon rosemary
1/4 cup of flour

Prior to cooking venison liver check to see that it is not speckled with white spots. This can be done in the field when the carcass is being emptied. If such white spots are observed, discard liver. Before cooking, liver should be soaked in a salt water solution for several hours or overnight. Remove from water and, after drying the meat, wrap in waxed paper and place in the freezer until it is nearly frozen. This will facilitate cutting the meat into relatively thin slices. Slice meat. Allow meat to reach room temperature. Mix seasoning with flour. Dredge meat in the mixture and fry in cooking oil on medium heat until desired degree of tenderness is reached. Serves 4

IN THE 1920S THERE WERE 500,000 WHITE-TAILED DEER IN THE U.S.; TODAY THERE ARE 18,000,000. IN THE 1920S THERE WERE 100,000 ELK; TODAY THERE ARE 900,000.

Basic Venison Stock

Calories: 0

Pro: 0

Fat: 0

CHO: 0

Diabetic Exchanges:

Lean Meat: 0

Vegetable: 0

Bread: 0

3 pounds venison bones
1 1/2 pounds meat scraps
3 celery ribs with leaves
1 large onion, chopped
2 large carrots, chopped
6 sprigs parsley
2 cloves

1 bay leaf
1 teaspoon thyme
8 peppercorns
4 juniper berries, crushed
4 quarts cold water
salt and pepper to taste

Place all ingredients in a large stock/soup pot and bring to a boil. Skim any foam rising to the top. Turn down heat and simmer partially covered for 2 hours. Remove meat and bones and cook uncovered for an additional 1 1/2 hours. Strain the stock through a large sieve. Cool to room temperature and refrigerate. Before use, remove any fat that has hardened on the surface of the liquid. Stock can be frozen for later use.

GROUND VENISON

Venison Helper

Calories: 269
Pro: 37
Fat: 9
CHO: 9

Diabetic Exchanges:
Lean Meat: 4
Vegetable: 0
Bread: 1/2

1 pound ground venison
2 tablespoons ketchup
1 can cream of mushroom soup
1/2 cup water

1/2 cup fresh onion, chopped
2 teaspoons hot mustard
1/2 teaspoons salt

Brown meat and onion in a skillet. Stir in remaining ingredients and simmer 30 minutes. Serve over rice or pasta. Serves 4.

Venison Dip

Calories: 448
Pro: 52
Fat: 17
CHO: 29

Diabetic Exchanges:
Lean Meat: 5
Vegetable: 0
Bread: 2 (without chips)

2 pounds ground venison
2 cans refried beans with green chilies
1 pound grated sharp cheddar cheese

1 large jar of salsa

Brown ground venison in iron skillet. Add the refried beans, salsa, and cheddar cheese and heat in crock pot. Serve with corn chips. Serves 4-6.

DEER HAVE A COMMON ORIGIN WITH GIRAFFES, GOING BACK 6 MILLION YEARS.

Venison Meatloaf

Calories: 262

Pro: 39

Fat: 6

CHO: 12

Diabetic Exchanges:

Lean Meat: 4

Vegetable: 0

Bread: 1/2

2 pounds ground venison

3/4 cups rolled oats (barley or rice may be used)

2 eggs

1/2 cup tomato paste

1 teaspoon salt

1/2 cup chopped sweet onion

1 cup tomato juice

1/2 teaspoon black pepper

Mix ingredients, fold into a large loaf pan, bake 1 1/2 hours at 325 degrees. Serves 8.

Ground Venison In Cabbage Leaves

Calories: 206

Pro: 36

Fat: 4

CHO: 6

Diabetic   Exchanges:

Lean Meat: 3

Vegetable: 0

Bread: 1/2

8 large cabbage leaves

3 tablespoons onion, finely chopped

1/2 teaspoon thyme

1/8 teaspoon cayenne pepper

1 pound ground venison

3/4 teaspoon salt

1/2 mashed clove garlic

1/2 cup tomato sauce

Wash and parblanch the cabbage leaves, drain and dry them on a towel. Brown venison well in a medium hot frying pan. Combine onion, thyme, cayenne pepper, venison, salt and mashed garlic. Spoon mixture onto individual cabbage leaves and roll or fold over. Place cabbage rolls in a heavy skillet and cover with tomato sauce. Simmer 10 minutes. Serves 4.

Venison Meat Loaf

Calories: 503
Pro: 47
Fat: 23
CHO: 26

Diabetic Exchanges:
Lean Meat: 5
Skim Milk: 1
Bread: 1
  Fat: 2

1 pound ground venison
1/3 pound ground pork
1 cup ketchup
1 1/2 teaspoons salt

1/2 cup rolled oats
1 egg
1/3 cup onion, chopped
1/4 cup milk

After mixing the meats together thoroughly, add salt, rolled oats, egg, chopped onion and milk. Place in loaf pan and bake for 1 hour in a medium oven at 350 degrees. Serves 4.

Savory Venison Pie

Calories: 207
Pro: 20
Fat: 4
CHO: 21

Diabetic Exchanges:
Lean Meat: 2
Vegetable: 0
Bread: 1-1/2

1 pound ground venison
1/2 teaspoon garlic powder
salt and pepper
3 large potatoes thinly sliced
2 tablespoons Worcestershire sauce

1 large onion, chopped
1/2 teaspoon dried oregano
1 can water
1 can cream of chicken soup

Mix meat, onion, seasonings and Worcestershire. Press into 9 x 13 baking dish. Top with sliced potatoes. Mix cream of chicken soup with water. Pour over potatoes. Cover and bake for 1 hour at 350 degrees. Serves 6 to 8.

Venison Burger Surprise

Calories: 320
Pro: 39
Fat: 4
CHO: 32

Diabetic Exchanges:
Lean Meat: 4
Vegetable: 0
Bread: 2

1 1/2 pound ground venison
1/2 tablespoon salt
1/4 tablespoon pepper
sliced cheese (optional)

1 medium onion
1/2 tablespoon garlic powder
English muffins

Mix ground venison, salt, pepper, and garlic powder; make approximately 6 patties. Broil until almost done, and add sliced onions and place patties and onion (cheese) between muffins. Broil until done.

Venison Meatballs

Calories: 44
Pro: 4
Fat: 3
CHO: 0

Diabetic Exchanges:
Lean Meat: 1/2
Vegetable: 0
Bread: 0

1 pound ground venison
1/8 tablespoon garlic juice or 1/2 tablespoon garlic salt
salt and pepper
1 pint sour cream

1 cup deviled ham

margarine
1 tablespoon horseradish

Mix ground venison, deviled ham, garlic juice, salt and pepper and shape into small balls. Brown in small amount of margarine. Heat sour cream and horseradish over low heat, and add meatballs. Serve on toothpicks. Allows for approximately 40 meatballs.

Venison Loaf

Calories: 254
Pro: 38
Fat: 5
CHO: 15

Diabetic Exchanges:
Lean Meat: 3
Vegetable: 0
Bread: 1

2/3 cup milk
1/2 cup soft bread crumbs
1/4 cup green pepper, chopped
1/2 cup onion, chopped

1 egg beaten
1 1/2 pound ground venison
1/4 cup ketchup
2 tablespoons salt

Blend all ingredients and place in baking dish or loaf pan. Bake at 350 degrees for 1 hour. Makes 4-6 servings.

Cocktail Meatballs

Calories: 54
Pro: 4
Fat: 2
CHO: 5

Diabetic Exchanges:
Lean Meat: 1/2
Vegetable: 0
Bread: 1/2

2 pounds ground venison
1 teaspoon Worcestershire sauce
1 medium onion, chopped
3 slices bread, cubed
1/4 cup milk
12 ounce jar grape jelly

2 eggs, beaten
1/2 pound pork sausage
1 teaspoon salt
pepper to taste
cooking oil
1 bottle chili sauce

Mix all ingredients except jelly & chili sauce, together and roll into 1/2 to 1 inch balls and lightly fry for about 4 or 5 minutes. Mix 1 bottle chili sauce and 12 ounces grape jelly over medium heat until jelly dissolves. Pour over meatballs and let simmer or put in crockpot on low, stirring occasionally until warmed through. Makes approximately 80 meatballs.

French Canadian Wild Game Holiday Pie

Calories: 475
Pro: 29
Fat: 24
CHO: 30

Diabetic Exchanges:
Medium Fat Meat: 3
Fat: 2
Bread: 2

1/2 pound ground venison
1 teaspoon course black pepper
1 small onion, chopped
1 cup water
1 1/2 cups mashed potatoes
1 teaspoon salt
1 pound ground lean pork
1/2 teaspoon cinnamon
1/8 teaspoon crushed cloves
1 ready made pie crust, bottom and top shell

Simmer venison, pork and onion in a large pot until the meat is light brown. Add the rest of the ingredients to the pot and simmer for 40 minutes. Pour ingredients into the pie shell, cover with the top shell, trim excess material, and punch holes in the top shell with a fork to vent. Bake at 400 degrees for 45 minutes. Serves 6-8.

DEER WILL SHY AWAY FROM AN UNKNOWN SIGHT OR SMELL, BUT WILL OFTEN INVESTIGATE, VERY CAREFULLY, AN UNKNOWN SOUND.

Broccoli Venison Squares

Calories: 330
Pro: 16
Fat: 19
CHO: 25

Diabetic Exchanges:
Medium Fat Meat: 2
Vegetable: 0
Bread: 2
Fat: 1

2 cups fresh broccoli, chopped
1 pound ground venison
1 4 ounce can mushroom stems and pieces, drained
1/4 cup Parmesan cheese
1/2 teaspoon salt
2 cups shredded Cheddar cheese
dash of pepper

2 cups Bisquick
1/2 cup cold water
4 eggs
1/2 cup milk
2 tablespoons peanut oil
1/3 cup onion, chopped

Heat oven to 400 degrees. Grease 13 x 9 baking dish. In a sauce pan heat about one inch of salted water to boiling, add broccoli, cover and cook for about 5 minutes or until not quite tender. Remove and drain thoroughly. In a skillet add the peanut oil and brown the ground venison, remove and drain. In a mixing bowl combine the meat, mushrooms, 1-1/2 cups Cheddar cheese and onion. Mix the Bisquick, water and remaining Cheddar cheese until a soft dough forms. Pat the dough in the greased baking dish with floured hands, pressing 1/2 inch up the sides. Spread the venison mixture over the dough, sprinkle with broccoli. Mix remaining ingredients and pour over broccoli. Bake until knife can be inserted and comes out clean, about 25-30 minutes. Serves 6-8.

Stuffed Tomatoes

Calories: 187
Pro: 19
Fat: 8
CHO: 8

Diabetic Exchanges:
Lean Meat: 2
Vegetable: 1
Bread: 1/2

8 tomatoes, ripe
1 pound ground venison
3 tablespoons cooking oil or butter
6 tablespoons rice, cooked/instant
1 medium onion, chopped fine

1/4 cup dry white wine
1/4 cup water
2 cloves garlic, chopped
1 small can tomato juice
1/4 cup parsley, chopped

Wash tomatoes, cut the tops off, leaving an opening and save the top for a cap. With a small spoon, scoop out the pulp and save in a bowl. Arrange tomato shells in a baking dish. To prepare stuffing, heat oil in skillet and add onions. Cook over moderate heat until soft and transparent, then add the garlic and parsley and blend. Add the ground venison, mashing with a fork, add wine and water. Cover and simmer for 4-5 minutes. Add the rice and tomato pulp and stir all together. It may be necessary to add some tomato juice as the rice will absorb a good deal of liquid. Cover skillet and simmer for about 7 minutes, then salt and pepper to taste. Remove from heat and fill the tomato shells about 2/3 full with the stuffing and the liquid. Replace the tomato caps and brush lightly with oil. Bake at 350 degrees about 1 hour, basting several times with the liquid that will accumulate in the bottom of the dish. Serves 8.

Hot Deer Dip

Calories: 261
Pro: 24
Fat: 16
CHO: 7

Diabetic Exchanges:
Lean Meat: 3
Vegetable: 1
Fat (without chips): 1

1 pound ground venison, cubed
1/4 cup green peppers, chopped
4 ounce can green chilies, chopped
2 tablespoons chili powder
1 pound pasteurized process cheese spread
2 tablespoons Worcestershire sauce
1/3 cup ripe olives, chopped
1/4 can jalapeno relish
1 medium onion, chopped
1 tomato, chopped
salt to taste

Brown the ground venison and the onion in a frying pan until the meat is crumbly. Drain off any drippings. Add the cheese, stirring while it melts. Stir in the rest of the ingredients and mix well. Transfer to a crock pot or fondue pot and serve warm with corn chips. Serves 8-10.

Venison Meatballs

Calories: 278
Pro: 41
Fat: 12
CHO: 2

Diabetic   Exchanges:
Lean Meat: 5
Vegetable: 0
Bread: 0

1 pound venison, ground
1/2 cup onion, chopped
1/2 cup Parmesan cheese
1/2 cup green pepper
1 large egg
1 teaspoon garlic, chopped
1/4 teaspoon sweet basil
1/4 teaspoon oregano
1/4 cup olive oil
salt and pepper to taste

Put all ingredients except the olive oil in a large bowl. Mix well with your hands and shape into golf ball size meat balls. Pour olive oil into a large skillet and brown at medium heat and cook until done through. Remove and drain on a paper towel. Serve with sauce of your choice over pasta. Serves 4.

Stuffed Pasta Shells

Calories: 518

Pro: 49

Fat: 14

CHO: 50

Diabetic Exchanges:

Lean Meat: 5

Vegetable: 0

Bread: 3

1 1/2 pound ground venison

1 large onion, chopped

1 clove garlic, chopped

8 ounces mushroom, sliced

1/4 cup parsley flakes

2 eggs

dash of salt and pepper

1 1/2 cup Parmesan cheese

1/2 cup bread crumbs

2 tablespoons olive oil

12 ounce package pasta shells to stuff

1 8 ounce package grated Mozzarella cheese

1 large jar prepared spaghetti sauce

In a large skillet over medium heat add olive oil, venison, onions, garlic and mushrooms. Cool and mix the bread crumbs, parsley flakes, eggs, salt, pepper and Parmesan cheese. Cook the pasta shells according to directions on package. Cool, stuff with meat mixture and put in a 9 x 13 baking dish. Cover with spaghetti sauce. Over the top sprinkle with 8 ounces grated Mozzarella cheese. Bake at 350 degrees for 30 to 40 minutes. This recipe can be made ahead of time and either refrigerated for the next day or frozen until later. Serves 6-8

Venison Stuffed Cabbage

Calories: 101
Pro: 9
Fat: 3
CHO: 9

Diabetic Exchanges:
Lean Meat: 1
Vegetable: 0
Bread: 1/2

1 pound ground venison
1 teaspoon Worcestershire sauce
salt and pepper to taste
dash of Tabasco or hot sauce
1 16 ounce can of seasoned tomatoes
2/3 cup of uncooked rice

2 tablespoons peanut oil
1 large head cabbage
1 large onion, chopped
1 8 ounce can tomato sauce

Par boil cabbage head in salted water for about 5 minutes or until soft. Core and remove outside leaves. These leaves can be used for garnish on the finished dish if desired. In a separate pan, cook the rice according to directions using the water in which the cabbage was boiled. In a skillet heat the oil and brown the venison, add salt, pepper and onion. Then add rice, tomato sauce, Worcestershire sauce and Tabasco or hot sauce. Mix well. Lay each leaf out flat and spoon on some of the meat mixture. Fold over top and bottom of each leaf and roll into a cylindrical shape. Place in the bottom of a baking dish with the final rolled flap on the bottom side. Pour seasoned tomatoes over the cabbage rolls, cover and bake at 350 degrees for 1 hour. This should make 18 to 20 rolls depending upon how much filling you use in each one.

> IN NORMAN TIMES, THE POSSESSION OF LARGE "DEER PARKS," AND THE EATING OF VENISON WAS PROOF OF HIGH SOCIAL STATUS.

Pizza Casserole

Calories: 468
Pro: 42
Fat: 10
CHO: 52

Diabetic Exchanges:
Lean Meat: 4
Vegetable: 0
Bread: 3

1 pound egg noodles
1-1/2 pounds ground venison
1/2 cup onions, chopped
1/4 cup green pepper, chopped
1/4 cup celery, chopped
8 ounces grated Mozzarella cheese
1/2 teaspoon pepper

1/2 teaspoon salt
1/2 teaspoon oregano
1/4 can mushrooms
1 8 ounce can pizza sauce
1 can tomato soup
1 teaspoon garlic salt

Cook the egg noodles according to directions and set aside. In a hot skillet, place about 2 tablespoons of cooking oil and brown the ground venison, onion, green pepper and celery. Drain and add the seasonings and all other ingredients except the cheese in the skillet and mix thoroughly. In a baking dish or casserole, arrange two layers consisting of first, the egg noodles, then the meat/sauce mix and sprinkle with Mozzarella cheese. Repeat for second layer. Bake in 350 degrees oven for 35 minutes. Serves 6-8.

In 1993 hunters paid $492 million in license fees. The vast majority of these fees went to some level of wildlife management programming.

Venison Meatloaf

Calories: 218
Pro: 26
Fat: 9
CHO: 8

Diabetic Exchanges:
Lean Meat: 3
Vegetable: 0
Bread: 1/2

1-1/2 pounds venison, ground
1/2 pound mild pork sausage
3/4 cup rolled oats, uncooked
1/4 cup onion, chopped
1/4 teaspoon garlic salt

1- 1/4 cup tomato juice
1 egg
1 teaspoon salt
1/4 teaspoon pepper

Mix all the ingredients well being sure there is a good blend of the pork and the venison. Pack into an ungreased 8-1/2 x 4-1/2 x 2-1/2 inch loaf pan and bake for about 1 1/2 hours. Let stand on top of the stove for several minutes before cutting. Serves 8-10.

Pepperoni Sticks

Calories: 54
Pro: 8
Fat: 2
CHO: 0

Diabetic Exchanges:
Lean Meat: 1
Vegetable: 0
Bread: 0

1 pound ground venison, lean
1/2 teaspoon crushed fennel seeds
1/2 teaspoon mustard seeds
1/4 teaspoon crushed red pepper
3/4 teaspoon freshly ground black pepper

1/4 pound hot pork sausage
1/4 teaspoon anise seeds
1 teaspoon liquid smoke
1/4 teaspoon garlic powder

Put everything in a large bowl and mix it using your hands. Be sure all the ingredients are completely blended together. Separate into two parts. Roll each half into long sticks about an 1 1/2 inches in diameter. Wrap each stick in aluminum foil and leave it in the refrigerator over night. The next day, unwrap the meat, place it on a broiler pan and bake for about 4 hours at 200 degrees. Additional cooking will result in a dryer stick, so bake to suit your taste. The sticks should be kept wrapped in the refrigerator until they are eaten.

Meat Loaf

Calories: 371
Pro: 36
Fat: 13
CHO: 25

Diabetic Exchanges:
Lean Meat: 4
Vegetable: 0
Bread: 2

1 1/2 pound ground venison, lean
1/3 cup onion, chopped
1/4 cup ketchup
2 cups soft bread crumbs
2 teaspoons commercial sausage seasoning

1/2 pound ground pork
1/4 cup whole milk
2 eggs
1 teaspoon salt

Mix everything in a large bowl being sure that it is well blended. Shape into a loaf and either place in a greased 9x5x3 inch pan or in a greased baking dish. At 350 degrees, bake for 1 hour and 15 minutes. After removing from oven, let loaf sit for about 10 minutes before slicing and serving. As the main meat, this should serve about 6 or 8 persons.

IN **1993** THE EXCISE TAXES ON SPORTING EQUIPMENT PAID BY HUNTERS WAS **$182** MILLION.

Venison Salami

Calories: 69
Pro: 11
Fat: 2
CHO: 0

Diabetic Exchanges:
Lean Meat: 1
Vegetable: 0
Bread: 0

1 pound ground venison
1 teaspoon salt
1/8 teaspoon nutmeg
1/2 teaspoon mustard seeds

1 tablespoon olive oil
dash of liquid smoke
1/2 teaspoon garlic powder

Mix everything in a large bowl being sure that it is well blended. Separate into two parts. Roll each half into long sticks about an 1 1/2 inches in diameter. Wrap each stick in aluminum foil and leave it in the refrigerator over night. The next day, unwrap the meat, place it on a broiler pan and bake for about 4 hours at 200 degrees. Additional cooking will result in a dryer stick, so bake to suit your taste. The stick should be kept individually wrapped in the refrigerator until used.

Venison Meatballs With Sauce

Calories: 32 per meatball
Pro: 3
Fat: 1
CHO: 2

Diabetic Exchanges:
Lean Meat: 1
Vegetable: 0
Bread: 0

1 1/2 pound ground venison
2 cups potatoes, grated
2/3 cup chopped onions
1 1/2 teaspoons salt
3 cups water

1/4 cup milk
1 egg
1/4 teaspoon pepper
1/4 cup butter or margarine
3 tablespoons flour

2 cups sour cream   *1 teaspoon dillweed*
10-ounce package frozen peas, cooked

Combine venison, potatoes, onions, salt, pepper, milk and egg in a bowl and mix well. Shape mixture into 1 1/2 inch balls. Melt butter and brown meat balls slowly on all sides in a heavy skillet. Add 1/2 cup water, cover and simmer for 20 minutes. Remove meat balls and keep warm. Blend flour with 1/2 cup of the water and stir into liquid in the skillet. Add the remaining water. Stirring constantly, cook over low heat until thickened and smooth. Bring sauce to a boil over high heat until it is reduced by about one-third. Reduce the heat and slowly stir in the sour cream and dill weed. Add the meat balls and the peas and reheat to a serving temperature without boiling. Makes approximately 80 meat balls.

FOR SOME UNKNOWN REASON, THE HAIR ON THE BRISKET OF A DEER POINTS FORWARD. ALL THE OTHER HAIR ON THE BODY POINTS REARWARD OR DOWN.

Venison Mincemeat

Calories 232:
Pro: 8
Fat: 8
CHO: 32

Diabetic Exchanges:
Lean Meat: 1
Fruit: 2
Bread: 1

2 cups venison, finely chopped (can use flank or neck)
Liquid to cover (broth, cider, vinegar or sweet cider)
1 tablespoon ground nutmeg   1 teaspoon ground cloves
2 cups tart apples, peeled, chopped 2 cups sugar
2 teaspoons salt   1 cup ground suet
1 pound currants   1/2 pound citron, chopped
1 tablespoon ground cinnamon   1 cup candied mixed fruits
1 pound raisins

Mix ingredients thoroughly. Bring to a boil and simmer for 15 minutes, stirring frequently. This recipe will make about 7 pints of mincemeat. 1 pint will make one pie. Serves 6-8 per pie.

Venison Bolognese

Calories: 150
Pro: 17
Fat: 4
CHO: 8

Diabetic Exchanges:
Lean Meat: 2
Vegetable: 1
Bread: 0

1/4 teaspoon crushed red pepper   1 tablespoon olive oil
1 small onion, chopped fine   1/2 pound ground venison
1/2 cup dry red wine   1 teaspoon sugar
2 tablespoons tomato paste   1 teaspoon dried oregano
1/2 teaspoon dried rosemary   1 bay leaf
1 16 ounce can salt free whole tomatoes
1 tablespoon finely shredded basil leaves
1 tablespoon finely chopped Italian parsley

In a large skillet, heat oil, add venison, onion, garlic and pepper flakes. Saute for 8 minutes or until tender. Add wine, deglaze pan, add tomatoes and stir in the remaining ingredients. Simmer until thick, about 25 minutes. Spoon over pasta to serve. Serves 4.

Block Party Beans

Calories: 380
Pro: 37
Fat: 3
CHO: 45

Diabetic Exchanges:
Lean Meat: 3
Vegetable: 2
Bread: 2

2 pounds ground venison
2 cups onion, chopped
1 cup celery, chopped
1 can 10 1/2 ounce tomato soup
1 can 6 ounce tomato paste
1/2 cup ketchup
1 pound green beans

17 ounces lima beans
15 ounces yellow wax beans
15 ounces can chili beans
1 pound can pork and beans
1/2 cup brown sugar
2 tablespoons mustard

Put about a tablespoon of cooking oil into a large skillet and brown the ground venison. Add onion and celery and cook until tender. Stir in soup, tomato paste and ketchup. Simmer 15 - 20 minutes. Pour contents of skillet into either a crockpot or a large baking dish. Drain green, wax and lima beans and add to pot/dish. Pork and beans and chili beans are added next, but do not drain. Add the liquid that is in the can. Add brown sugar and mustard. Stir, combining thoroughly all ingredients. Bake uncovered in 325 degree oven for 1 hour or in a crockpot until the beans are cooked through. Serves 12.

THERE ARE 53 SPECIES OF DEER IN THE WORLD.

Creole Patties

Calories: 200
Pro: 23
Fat: 8
CHO: 7

Diabetic Exchanges:
Lean Meat: 3
Vegetable: 0
Bread: 1/2

2 pounds ground venison
1/2 teaspoon powdered bay leaf
1/2 pound ground veal
1/4 cup flour
2 teaspoons salt
1/2 teaspoon black pepper
1/4 teaspoon thyme

1/4 teaspoon marjoram
1/2 pound ground pork
1/4 teaspoon allspice
1/2 teaspoon nutmeg
3/4 cup onion, chopped
2 cloves garlic, minced
1/4 cup peanut oil

In a large mixing bowl place all the ingredients, except the oil. Mix together thoroughly with your hands until well blended in texture. Shape into serving size patties. Heat the oil in large skillet and fry over low heat. Cooking time depends on how thick the patties are made, but don't overcook. Makes 10-12 patties.

Venison Tacos

Calories: 334
Pro: 28
Fat: 13
CHO: 24

Diabetic Exchanges:
Lean Meat: 4
Vegetable: 1
Bread: 1

1 1/2 pounds ground venison
1/2 teaspoon salt
3 tablespoons ketchup
1 clove garlic, finely chopped
1 1/2 tablespoons chili powder
2 tablespoons Worcestershire sauce

1 cup cold water
1/2 teaspoon pepper
1 medium onion, chopped
2 tablespoons olive oil
1 package taco seasoning mix

In a cast iron skillet, brown the meat, onions and garlic in the olive oil. Drain off all liquid. Mix the taco seasoning mix, ketchup, Worcestershire sauce and chili powder in the cup of cold water. Add the meat mixture and bring to a boil, then simmer, uncovered, for 20 minutes, stirring frequently, until medium thick consistency is reached. Add additional water if necessary. Pour sauce into warm taco shells and add grated cheddar cheese, shredded lettuce, chopped tomatoes and taco sauce. Makes 12 tacos.

Spanish Rice

Calories: 330
Pro: 38
Fat: 9
CHO: 20

Diabetic Exchanges:
Lean Meat: 4
Vegetable: 1
Bread: 1

6 slices of bacon
1 1/2 pound ground venison
1 cup uncooked rice
1 28 ounce can tomato juice

1 medium onion, chopped
1/2 teaspoon salt
1 teaspoon paprika

Cook bacon, remove from the pan, then brown onions and venison in 2 tablespoons of the bacon grease. Add salt, rice, canned tomatoes and paprika. Cover and cook on low heat 30 minutes. Add tomato juice as necessary until rice is tender.

CONTRARY TO MANY OTHER ANIMALS, WHITETAILS HAVE TWICE AS MUCH HAIR IN THE SUMMER THAN IN THE WINTER.

Venison Helper

Calories: 271
Pro: 36
Fat: 9
CHO: 6

Diabetic Exchanges:
Lean Meat: 4
Vegetable: 0
Bread: 1/2

1 pound ground venison
2 tablespoons ketchup
1 can cream of mushroom soup
1/2 cup water
1/2 cup fresh onion
2 teaspoons hot mustard
1/2 teaspoon salt

Brown meat and onion in a skillet. Stir in remaining ingredients and simmer 30 minutes. Serve over rice or pasta.

Venison Mushroom Patties

Calories: 160
Pro: 24
Fat: 5
CHO: 4

Diabetic Exchanges:
Lean Meat: 3
Vegetable: 1
Bread: 0

2 pounds venison (ground, lean)
garlic salt
1/4 tablespoon pepper
1/4 cup cooking oil
1 tablespoon Worcestershire
1 cup milk
1 tablespoon salt
1/4 cup flour
1 cup cream of
    mushroom soup

Mix meat, 1/2 cup milk and seasoning in bowl. Make into patties and roll in flour; brown in oil in skillet. Brown on both sides and drain off fat; add soup and remaining 1/2 cup milk. Cover and cook on low heat for approximately 15 minutes or until done. Serves 10-12

Venison Lasagne

Calories: 380
Pro: 25
Fat: 13
CHO: 40

Diabetic Exchanges:
Medium Fat Meat: 3
Vegetable: 0
Bread: 2

Sauce:
2 tablespoons olive oil
1 large onion, diced
1 28 ounce can tomatoes
1/4 teaspoon oregano
1/4 teaspoon rosemary
1 28 ounce jar prepared pasta sauce

1 pound ground venison
1/2 pound mushrooms, sliced
1 teaspoon of garlic powder
1/4 teaspoon fennel
3 bay leaves

Filling:
1 cup grated parmesan cheese   2 eggs slightly beaten
2 16 ounce containers ricotta cheese
3 cups (12 ounces) shredded mozzarella cheese
16 ounces lasagne, cooked and drained

Prepare meat sauce: Brown venison and onion in olive oil. Add remaining sauce ingredients. Bring to boil, reduce heat, cover and simmer at least 30 minutes. **Preparing filling:** Combine ricotta, eggs, 2 1/4 cups of the mozzarella, and 3/4 cups of parmesan. **To Assemble:** Add one cup of meat sauce in a 13"X 9" X 2" baking dish. Cover with lasagne and spread 1/3 of the ricotta mixture. Repeat layering meat sauce, lasagne, ricotta mixture with remaining ingredients. Top with remaining 3/4 cups mozzarella and 3/4 cup parmesan. Cover and bake at 375 degrees for 40 minutes. Uncover and bake until brown. Serves 12.

Kennesaw Meat Loaf

Calories: 270
Pro: 30
Fat: 12
CHO: 9

Diabetic Exchanges:
Lean Meat: 4
Vegetable: 0
Bread: 1/2

1/4 pound pork sausage
1 pound ground venison
1 egg
1 tablespoon bread crumbs

1 envelope dry onion soup mix
1 teaspoon pepper
2 teaspoons basil
1 cup evaporated milk

Preheat oven to 350 degrees. Mix all ingredients together and shape into 4 loaves. Place loaves in a 9 x 11 inch metal baking pan. Bake for 35-40 minutes.

Venison Loaf in a Blanket

Calories: 495
Pro: 46
Fat: 18
CHO: 35

Diabetic Exchanges:
Lean Meat: 4
Fat: 2
Bread: 2

1 medium chopped onion
2 cups cubed cooked potatoes
2 eggs
salt
1 package pre-made
   pie crust dough

6 strips of lean bacon
1 1/2 pounds ground venison
1/2 cup milk
pepper

Cook bacon and brown onions in reserved drippings. Add crumbled bacon and onions to the cooked potatoes. Brown the venison and add to the potato mixture. Add eggs, milk, salt, pepper, mix and heat thoroughly. Shape mixture into a loaf and wrap with pie crust dough. Seal seams by pinching dough together. Place seam side down on a lightly greased baking sheet. Cook at 425 degrees 15 to 20 minutes, until crust is golden brown. Serves 6.

Cranberry Venison Loaf

Calories: 370
Pro: 42
Fat: 8
CHO: 35

Diabetic Exchanges:
Lean Meat: 4
Skim Milk: 1/2
Bread: 1

2 pounds ground venison
2 eggs well beaten
1/4 teaspoon black pepper
3/4 cup seasoned bread crumbs
1 16 ounce can whole cranberry sauce

3/4 cup milk
1 1/2 teaspoons salt
1 teaspoon sweet basil
1/4 cup brown sugar

Combine brown sugar and cranberry sauce and spread over the bottom of a greased loaf pan. Combine the remaining ingredients and shape into a loaf. Place loaf into loaf pan. Bake at 350 for one hour. Serves 8.

WHITETAILS IN A PEN IN NEW JERSEY,

JUMPED A FENCE SLIGHTLY OVER NINE

FEET IN HEIGHT — FROM BOTH A

RUNNING AND STANDING POSITION.

Deer Dip

Calories: 219
Pro: 17
Fat: 15
CHO: 6

Diabetic Exchanges:
Medium Fat Meat: 2
Vegetable: 1
Bread: 1/2

1/2 pound ground venison
1 can salsa

1 16 ounce Velvetta cheese

Brown deer meat in skillet and drain. Add cheese and salsa. Warm over low heat. Serves 8-10.

Venison Chili

Calories: 447
Pro: 48
Fat: 11
CHO: 40

Diabetic Exchanges:
Lean Meat: 4
Vegetable: 2
Bread: 2

2 teaspoons chili powder
1 1/4 red pepper
1/2 cup red wine
1 cup baby lima beans
1 teaspoon dried marjoram, or oregano
2 pounds venison shoulder, cut in 1/2" cubes
1 16 ounce can dark red kidney beans, drained
1 1/2 beef broth or chicken broth
1/4 pound slab of bacon, cut 1/4" dice
1 medium onion, chopped coarsely
6 medium carrots, cut in 1/2" slices

2 teaspoons cumin
1 28 ounce tomatoes
1/4 cup tomato paste
3 cups rice or barley, cooked

Brown bacon in skillet. Remove bacon and set aside. Reserve 3 tablespoons bacon fat. Place 2 tablespoons bacon fat in a casserole dish. Add onions and carrots. Sprinkle chili powder/marjoram.

Add reserved bacon. Pour remaining bacon fat into skillet. Brown venison over medium heat. Add tomatoes, broth, wine and tomato paste. Bring to a simmer and cook uncovered for 40 minutes stirring occasionally. Add kidney beans, lima beans. Simmer 10 minutes until meat is tender. Serves 6. Serve over rice or barley.

Venison Meatloaf

Calories: 319

Pro: 40

Fat: 6

CHO: 25

Diabetic Exchanges:

Lean Meat: 4

Vegetable: 1

Bread: 1

3/4 cups rolled oats (barley or rice may be used)

2 pounds ground venison

2 eggs

1/2 cup tomato paste

1/2 cup chopped sweet onion

1 teaspoon salt

1 cup tomato juice

1/2 teaspoon black pepper

First mix ingredients, then fold into a large loaf pan, and bake 1 1/2 hours at 325 degrees.

NOTES

SAUSAGE

GENERAL INSTRUCTIONS FOR THE PREPARATION OF VENISON SAUSAGE

There are always lots of scrap pieces of good meat when you are finished cutting steaks, roasts and chops. There are also certain cuts that are not highly desirable for cooking as is. A perfect and delicious solution to this problem is sausage. It is easy to make, easy and quick to cook and very versatile.

Because venison is such a lean meat, some sort of fat or oil is added in any one of various ways to nearly every type of sausage recipe to compensate. In making sausage, the adding of fat not only satisfies the fat requirement but is a great addition to the flavor. It also acts as an extender, making your hard earned venison stretch over a lot more meals. The most common fat available is pork fat although beef fat can also be used. Always look for the hard fat that is found on the outside of the larger cuts of meat.

The proportions of fat to venison in making sausage are very important. When fat is added, it should be in a proportion of about 3 - 4 parts venison to each part fat. This is primarily because the sausage is almost always fried and if you fry the sausage to medium-well to well done, as many people do, it takes longer to cook a lot of fat than it does the lean venison and the sausage will be overcooked. If you add fat meat like fat pork shoulder and not just the fat alone, then the proportions can go to 1 - 1 or equal parts. In order to get the meat to cut cleanly and not get mushy, keep the meat itself as cold as possible. The stiffer it is, the better the consistency of the final sausage.

People are often deterred from making sausage because of the potential investment of a couple hundred dollars in an electric meat grinder that won't be used that often. There are several ways to beat that problem. You probably have several hunting friends who don't want to spend that kind of money either so you could perhaps split the cost four or five ways and share the machine. If you all get a deer within a week or two of each other, you could have a grinding party and do a big batch all at once. The only drawback to that is that everyone ends up with the same kind of sausage while some like it hot and others may like it on the mild side. There are two more reasonable answers. One is to locate an old-timey hand cranked meat grinder and just work at it a little harder. You use the medium cutter and feed the right proportions of meat and fat into the hopper and crank away. The seasonings are added to the ground meat and mixed in by hand.

For a little more investment, modern food processors are an even better answer. First, the cost is less than for the electric meat grinder. Secondly, the processor can be used for dozens of other kitchen tasks over the course of the year. Thirdly, seasonings, both dry and liquid, can be added to the meat, marinated overnight and then processed, thus getting more specific flavors into the final sausage. If you already have a favorite recipe, great. If not, you have some fun in store. You can create your own, exactly as you like it. Perhaps you want to duplicate a commercial brand. You can do that, too. What you do is to grind the meat (and fat product) and then shape a small patty, season the patty only, keeping track of what you added and in what quantity and proportions, and in a frying pan, cook it on the spot. If it seems to have to much of This and not enough of That, you can adjust the mix and try another. That way before you season the whole batch, you know you have what you want. The most common spices used are salt, pepper, ginger, sage, basil, thyme, garlic powder and ground allspice. Remember to keep good notes for next year.

Breakfast Sausage

Calories: 77
Pro: 10
Fat: 4
CHO: 2

Diabetic Exchanges:
Lean Meat: 1
Vegetable: 0
Bread: 0

8 slices of bacon
1 teaspoon sage
1/2 teaspoon salt

1 pound venison
1/4 teaspoon pepper

Cut the bacon slices about an inch wide across the grain and venison into 1/2 inch cubes. Place meat in a small bowl, mix salt, pepper and sage together, sprinkle over meat and mix well with your hands. Grind the mixture to desired consistency. Shape into patties and fry over a medium heat. Makes 16 patties.

Sausage

Calories: 68
Pro: 10
Fat: 3
CHO: 0

Diabetic Exchanges:
Lean Meat: 1
Vegetable: 0
Bread: 0

1 pound ground venison
1 teaspoon dry crushed oregano
1 teaspoon dry crushed basil
2 Tablespoons dry red wine
1/2 teaspoon mustard seeds
2 Tablespoons finely chopped onions

1/4 pound ground pork
1 teaspoon black pepper
1/4 teaspoon garlic powder
3 tablespoons grated Parmesan cheese

Mix everything in a large bowl being sure that it is well blended. Separate into several rolls or patties and leave in refrigerator until ready for frying. Makes 16 patties.

Mexican Sausage

(This sausage is spicy and can be used to make tacos, chili or other similar Mexican dishes.)

Calories: 145
Pro: 14
Fat: 9
CHO: 0

Diabetic Exchanges:
Lean Meat: 2
Vegetable: 0
Bread: 0

1 pound venison
1 tablespoon paprika
1/2 tablespoon black pepper
1/2 teaspoon garlic powder
2 tablespoons red wine vinegar

1 pound fatty pork, any cut
1 teaspoon salt
1 teaspoon cayenne pepper
1/4 teaspoon oregano

Cut the venison and pork into about 3/4 inch cubes and put into a mixing bowl. Sprinkle with all the dry ingredients and mix well with a large wooden spoon or fork. Grind to sausage consistency. Put the meat back into the mixing bowl, add the wine vinegar and mix well. Seal the bowl with foil or plastic wrap and put in the refrigerator for several of hours so the flavor of the vinegar soaks well into the meat. Either fry in patties or freeze for later use. Makes 16 patties.

Italian Garlic Sausage

Calories: 140

Pro: 15

Fat: 8

CHO: 0

Diabetic Exchanges:

Lean Meat: 2

Vegetable: 0

Bread: 0

1 pound venison

1 pound fatty pork, any cut

4 tablespoons fresh garlic, minced

1/2 cup water (or 1/4 cup rose wine and 1/4 cup water)

1 teaspoon salt

1 teaspoon pepper

Cut the venison and pork into about 3/4 inch cubes and put into a mixing bowl. Add salt, pepper and minced garlic and mix well. Grind to sausage consistency. Put the meat back into the mixing bowl, add the water or water/wine mixture and mix well. Seal the bowl tightly with foil or plastic wrap and put in the refrigerator for two days so the flavor of the garlic is more subtly and uniformly blended into the meat. Either fry in thin patties or freeze for later use. Makes 16 patties.

NOTES

NOTES

JERKY

General instructions for the preparation of venison jerky

Jerking meat is probably the oldest known method of preserving meats. In its simplest terms it means to dry the meat by removing the moisture content. The drier it is, the longer it will generally last. Keeping the finished product in a sealed container in the refrigerator is still the best storage technique even for the finished product.

Venison should have as much fat removed as is possible. Prior to cutting the meat, place it in the freezer until it is partially frozen. This will make the meat somewhat stiff and much easier to slice thinly. It can be cut in strips of any manageable length, but should be no more than 1/4 inch thick. Most people prefer it even a little thinner. If the meat is cut with the grain, after it is dried it will tend to be of the chewy variety. Cutting across the grain results in a more tender piece of meat that breaks off when you take a bite. Either method works well and is just a matter of preference. Another factor effecting the results is the length of time the meat is dried. The most common method is to place the strips of venison on a rack, not overlapping or layering, and drying it in a kitchen oven for 8 to 10 hours on the lowest possible setting (usually around 140 degrees) with the oven door ajar to allow the moisture to escape. Another possibility is placing the meat on racks in a smoker and drying it that way. If you use a smoker, remember that the purpose it to dry the meat, so don't introduce any kind of liquid into that process. Keep testing the meat after about 8 hours has gone by and take it out when it is the way you prefer it. There are many combinations of seasonings that can be used in making jerky. Some are dry and others are liquid. Both methods, however, involve allowing the meat to "marinate" for some period of time prior to cooking. If the marinade is dry, combine all the ingredients by stirring or mixing them well and generously sprinkle the mixture over the cut strips. If the marinade is in liquid form, pour over the meat. In both cases, after the marinade has been applied, place the meat in a sealed or tightly covered container and set it in the refrigerator. Since the meat is relatively thin, it doesn't take as long to marinate as do larger and thicker cuts. Six to ten hours is usually enough. Dry ingredient meat can then be put directly into the drying process. Liquid marinated meat should be drained in a colander before being put on the drying rack.

While jerking meat is a method of preservation, it won't last forever. After the drying process is completed and the jerky has cooled, store it in a tightly sealed container or airtight freezer bag in the refrigeration. That will definitely prolong it's life and should keep for a couple of months. If it's not handled that way, use it much sooner.

The following are several recipes that use either a dry or a liquid marinade. Since all the directions for preparation are the same no matter what the ingredients are, only the ingredients are listed.

Chili Jerky (dry)

Calories: (per ounce) 45

Pro: 7

Fat: trace

CHO: trace

Diabetic Exchanges:

Lean Meat: 1

Vegetable: 0

Bread: 0

1 pound venison, sliced no more than 1/4 inch thick

1/2 teaspoon garlic powder

1/2 teaspoon oregano, crushed

1 teaspoon salt

1 teaspoon chili powder

1 teaspoon paprika

1/4 teaspoon pepper

Mountain Jerky (liquid)

Calories: 45

Pro: 7

Fat: trace

CHO: trace

Diabetic Exchanges:

Lean Meat: 1

Vegetable: 0

Bread: 0

1 pound venison

4 tablespoons Worcestershire

1/4 teaspoon onion salt

1/4 teaspoon pepper

4 tablespoons soy sauce

1/4 teaspoon garlic powder

2 tablespoons ketchup

4 tablespoons sorghum or 2 tablespoons brown sugar

Desert Jerky (dry)

Calories: 45

Pro: 7

Fat: trace

CHO: trace

Diabetic Exchanges:

Lean Meat: 1

Vegetable: 0

Bread: 0

1 pound venison

1/8 teaspoon pepper

1/4 teaspoon ground ginger

1/4 teaspoon chili powder

1/8 teaspoon ground cumin

1/4 teaspoon turmeric

1 1/2 teaspoons coriander

1 teaspoon salt

Hot & Spicy Jerky (liquid)

Calories: 45
Pro: 7
Fat: trace
CHO: trace

Diabetic Exchanges:
Lean Meat: 1
Vegetable: 0
Bread: 0

1 pound venison
2 tablespoons A-1 Sauce
1/2 teaspoon paprika
1/4 teaspoon cayenne pepper
3 tablespoons Worcestershire sauce

1/4 teaspoon cracked pepper
2 cloves garlic, crushed
1 teaspoon onion powder
1 teaspoon salt

Barbecue Jerky (liquid)

Calories: 45
Pro: 7
Fat: trace
CHO: trace

Diabetic Exchanges:
Lean Meat: 1
Vegetable: 0
Bread: 0

1 pound venison
1/3 cup red wine vinegar
1 teaspoon dry mustard
1 teaspoon onion powder

3 tablespoons brown sugar
1/3 cup ketchup
1 /2 teaspoon garlic powder
1/8 teaspoon cayenne pepper

Old West Jerky (liquid)

Calories: 45
Pro: 7
Fat: trace
CHO: trace

Diabetic Exchanges:
Lean Meat: 1
Vegetable: 0
Bread: 0

1 pound venison
2 tablespoons liquid smoke
1 teaspoon salt
2 tablespoons Worcestershire sauce

1/4 teaspoon pepper
1 teaspoon garlic powder

Bombay Jerky (dry)

Calories: 45
Pro: 7
Fat: trace
CHO: trace

Diabetic Exchanges:
Lean Meat: 1
Vegetable: 0
Bread: 0

1 pound venison
1 1/2 teaspoons curry powder
1/8 teaspoon ginger
1/4 teaspoon pepper

1 teaspoon ground ginger
1/2 teaspoon garlic powder
1/8 teaspoon cinnamon
1/8 teaspoon ground cumin

Sweet and Sour Oriental Jerky

Calories: 45
Pro: 7
Fat: trace
CHO: trace

Diabetic Exchanges:
Lean Meat: 1
Vegetable: 0
Bread: 0

I pound venison
1/2 teaspoon onion powder
3 tablespoons brown sugar
1/4 cup red wine vinegar

1/4 teaspoon pepper
1 clove garlic, crushed
1 tablespoon soy sauce
1/4 cup pineapple juice

Coons Jerky

Calories: 45
Pro: 7
Fat: trace
CHO: trace

Diabetic Exchanges:
Lean Meat: 1
Vegetable: 0
Bread: 0

3 pounds venison
1/2 cup Worcestershire sauce
2 teaspoons seasoned salt
2 teaspoons onion powder

1/2 cup soy sauce
2 teaspoons Accent
2/3 teaspoon garlic powder
2/3 teaspoon black pepper

Venison Pemmican

Calories: 185

Pro: 7

Fat: 13

CHO: 13

Diabetic Exchanges:

Lean Meat: 1

Fruit: 1

Fat: 1

2 cups jerky (your favorite recipe) 1 1/2 cups of berries, dried 3/4 cup beef fat, bear fat or 1 1/2 sticks of butter

This is what the American Indians, the old Long Hunters and Mountain Men carried with them when they took their long walks. (Daniel Boone once "went deer hunting" for 14 months.) It should serve you well on your walking trips as well. Begin by making jerky with one of the recipes in this book or another of your favorites. It will have to be very well dried in order for the pemmican to come out right. The jerky needs to splinter and break when bent. The other main ingredient is some sort of berry. Possibilities are gooseberries, blueberries, cranberries or whatever else is at hand. Currants and tart red cherries can be used, too. You'll want to experiment. The berries also have to be very well dried. This can be simply done using the same method as drying jerky. Put the berries on a cookie sheet and dry them on the lowest heat in the oven. The dried berries can be stored in the refrigerator in a sealed plastic bag for later use if you want to dry a lot when they are in season. The jerky and the berries need to be pulverized into nearly a powder. This can be done either by literally pounding or in a food processor. Once you have the two blended together, melt the fat or butter and pour it into the mixture. If you're doing it by hand, have everything in a bowl so you can mix it. If you're working with a food processor, you can pour the fat right in and blend it. Immediately pour a one inch layer of the meat, berry, fat mixture into a baking pan and refrigerate. Once it is cold, the fat will have hardened and you can cut the finished product into the size square you wish to store. Storage should be in an air tight container if you intend to keep it a long time. When you carry it on your trek, keep it in an outside pocket in a sealed plastic bag. If you want to be historically correct, it can be carried wrapped in lint-free cloth or just loose. But don't take it to the beach and leave it in the sun to melt. Remember this is heavy stuff and that a little goes a long way so don't eat a pound of it at a time. Let it settle down before you eat a lot. It's probably a myth that it swells up in your stomach, but sometimes it might feel like it does. It is also possible to take a square(s) of pemmican, drop it in water and heat it to make a great trail soup.

GLOSSARY OF COOKING TERMS

Barbecue.................... Cooking (grill) over wood or charcoal fire while basting with a seasoned sauce.

Baste .... Preventing the drying of meat while cooking by brushing or pouring melted fat, oil, drippings or other liquids over the meat. This also adds a special flavor depending upon the liquid used.

Braise .... Browning meat in fat and then cooking, covered, in a small amount of liquid.

Bread .... Covering uncooked meat with a coating of some sort of crumbs.

Broil............................ Cooking meat quickly by use of direct dry heat, either open flame or an electric source of heat.

Cube .... Cutting into 1 or 2 inch pieces, usually square.

Dice............................. Cutting into small pieces, usually about a quarter of an inch square.

Dredge .... Dipping into and completely covering meat with flour.

Drippings .... The fat and other liquids that are cooked out of meat and accumulated in the bottom of a roasting or frying pan or pot.

Glaze........................... Coating meat with a special sauce or syrup, usually sweet.

Lard .... Either covering or inserting into the meat pieces of fat from another type of meat such as pork or beef. This adds the necessary moisture that venison lacks and, depending upon the fat used, imparts a slight flavor of its own.

Marinate .... Immersing meat in a special, seasoned liquid for a period of time. This has both a tenderizing effect and is a special flavor additive.

Panbroil .... Cooking meat in a dry skillet. Any fat or liquid produced by the meat itself, is poured off.

Panfry .... Cooking meat in a skillet with a little oil.

Parboil .... Partially or precooking meat (or vegetables), usually by boiling in water or light frying.

Poach .... Cooking slowly in liquid, (not quite boiling). Liquid should completely cover the meat.

Roast .... Cooking in an oven (dry heat), uncovered.

Saute .... Frying lightly in a small amount of oil.

Score .... Cutting shallow grooves or slashes in the surface of meat.

Sear .... Quickly browning meat by frying. The purpose is to seal in natural meat juices.

Simmer .... Cooking in liquid just below boiling.

Suet .... The solid white fat found on beef.

THE HUNGRY HUNTER VENISON COOKBOOK   123

THE EDITOR

James R. "Jim" Wilson, the editor of The Hungry Hunter series of cookbooks, the first volume of which is The Complete Venison Cookbook, has been a hunter and fisherman for many years both in the north and the south and a little in the west. He went through several colleges and universities, once as an English major and again later as a biology major. Then he married a french lady whose parents owned a hotel and restaurant on the outskirts of Paris where she learned her cooking skills. When Jim began bringing the game and fish

James R. Wilson

in from the field, the recipe experimentation and research began at home. Since then, it has been a constant search for the perfect game recipe. His favorite story concerns the day he was cooking "hamburgers" and served them to his two young daughters. After each of them had taken a bite, they looked at each other and wrinkled up their noses, complaining that "These hamburgers don't taste right". He had to explain to them that they were made with beef — not the venison they had grown up on. As the editor of Southern Wildlife magazine he came into contact with many other hunters and began to seek out and sort hundreds of venison recipes to compile for this book. While he added many of his own to this book, everyone who goes afield and returns with game has at least one special recipe that is worth passing on; most have considerably more. He chose the best for The Hungry Hunter.

NEED MORE COPIES OF THE HUNGRY HUNTER?

New! The perfect gift for the sportsman or woman.

❏ A unique and practical addition to your kitchen or hunting camp.

❏ Over 100 delicious recipes specifically developed for venison.

❏ Valuable information on nutrition & care and cooking of venison.

❏ Each recipe documented with protein, fat, and calorie information, along with diabetic exchange information.

❏ These beautiful, illustrated First Edition books can be autographed by the editor on request.

Each book is $14.95 plus $3.50 shipping and handling. Georgia Residents add 5% tax to total. Send check, money order, VISA or MasterCard (please include card number with expiration date with a signed order) & address to: The Hungry Hunter, Georgia Wildlife Press, 1930 Iris Drive, Conyers, Georgia, 30207. (Volume discounts available — Call 404-929-3350 for details.)

❏ MasterCard
❏ Visa
❏ Check Enclosed

How many cookbooks? _____ x $14.95 ea. = $ _____

+ Shipping & Handling Cost* _____

*$3.50 for first book, $1.50 for each additional book

+ Tax (5% in GA.) _____

= TOTAL _____

Name _____

Address _____

Card Number _____ exp. date _____

Signature _____ phone no.(___) _____

must be signed to use credit card

Mail Your Order To: The Hungry Hunter, Georgia Wildlife Press, 1930 Iris Drive, Conyers, Georgia, 30207

PHONE ORDERS CALL 404-929-3350